The ROI *of* Thought Leadership

CINDY
ANDERSON

ANTHONY
MARSHALL

FROM THE LEADERS OF IBM'S INSTITUTE FOR BUSINESS VALUE

The # ROI *of*
Thought
Leadership

**CALCULATING
THE VALUE THAT SETS
ORGANIZATIONS APART**

FOREWORD BY **BOB SAFIAN**
HOST AND EDITOR-AT-LARGE, RAPID RESPONSE

WILEY

Published by John Wiley & Sons, Inc., Hoboken, New Jersey.
Published simultaneously in Canada.

For general information on our other products and services or for technical support, please contact our Customer Care Department within the United States at (800) 762-2974, outside the United States at (317) 572-3993 or fax (317) 572-4002.

Wiley also publishes its books in a variety of electronic formats. Some content that appears in print may not be available in electronic formats. For more information about Wiley products, visit our web site at www.wiley.com.

Library of Congress Cataloging-in-Publication Data:

Names: Anderson, Cindy, author. | Marshall, Anthony (Director), author.
Title: The roi of thought leadership : Calculating the Value that Sets Organizations Apart / Cindy Anderson, Anthony Marshall.
Description: Hoboken, New Jersey : Wiley, [2025] | Includes index.
Identifiers: LCCN 2024038146 (print) | LCCN 2024038147 (ebook) | ISBN 9781394308910 (hardback) | ISBN 9781394308934 (adobe pdf) | ISBN 9781394308927 (epub)
Subjects: LCSH: Leadership.
Classification: LCC HD57.7 .A5255 2025 (print) | LCC HD57.7 (ebook) | DDC 658.4/092—dc23/eng/20240925
LC record available at https://lccn.loc.gov/2024038146
LC ebook record available at https://lccn.loc.gov/2024038147

COVER DESIGN: PAUL MCCARTHY
COVER IMAGERY: © GETTY IMAGES /
MARBLE: SEAN GLADWELL | GREEN PATH: ANDRIY ONUFRIYENKO

SKY10093733_121824

Contents

Foreword

As a journalist, I've always believed in the power of ideas. Truth matters. Facts matter. Insights matter. This is as true in business as in any arena. Understanding the world around us is the essential first step in any marketplace advance.

The irony is that proving this axiom – through facts and data – has been challenging. Unlike areas like technology and human resources and R&D, quantifying the return-on-investment of thought leadership has often been elusive.

That hasn't dampened the ardor of those of us committed to creating articles, analysis, reports, and graphics that illuminate misunderstood, underappreciated, and emerging topics. But it has made it more difficult to obtain resources, funding, and support for thought leadership. The positive impact of these efforts has been felt more than counted.

I've experienced this firsthand, throughout my career, as editor in chief of *Fast Company,* as an executive editor at *Time* and at *Fortune,* as the host of the *Rapid Response* podcast, and as a strategic advisor and managing director of The Flux Group. At each step of the way, compelling content has been rewarded with impact, with attention, often with prestige – but only rarely with commensurate dollars. Securing consistent budgetary support has been blunted by an inability to quantify return on investment (ROI) with business-like clarity.

When I heard that Cindy Anderson and Anthony Marshall, colleagues working together at IBM's Institute for Business Value, had decided to try bridging this divide and develop a system for quantifying the value of thought leadership, I thought, "Good luck!" Some things – often the most important things – just can't be measured.

But they were undaunted, and together they dedicated countless hours and brainpower to solving this conundrum. They conducted a series of anonymous double-blind surveys. They dug deep into numbers, avoiding leaps of fancy in favor of only the most prudent, conservative course. And to my great surprise – and great delight – they cracked it wide open.

This book presents research about thought leadership that is unique, eye-opening and entirely credible. Using both real-world data and clear, logical analysis, Marshall and Anderson demonstrate the value of thought leadership quantitatively. In essence, this book about thought leadership is itself thought leadership.

The book goes beyond generalities. It provides a formula for calculating any organization's specific thought leadership ROI. The book also provides rich lessons about what defines next-level thought leadership, how organizations can best improve their thought leadership impact, and how to build a balanced thought leadership portfolio. Anderson and Marshall dig into the importance of storytelling and how best to leverage communications channels in amplifying thought leadership. They unlock eight archetypes of thought leadership, and they explain how to target content and outreach for optimizing impact.

Our world today is awash in information. But the vast majority of that content is noise, distraction, misinformation.

True thought leadership is differentiated – it is credible and trusted; it is insightful and accurate; it builds reputation and prompts action that leads to results. For all of those reasons, true thought leadership is valuable, and it must be valued. In that way, this tool for measuring and managing the value of thought leadership is a universal gift. What Anderson and Marshall have done is give us all tools to support and safeguard work that improves our businesses and improves our world.

Robert Safian
Former *Fast Company* editor in chief
Host, *Rapid Response* podcast
Managing director, The Flux Group

Introduction

Many have long believed that thought leadership delivers business value, but no one has been able to prove it – until now.

Between 2021 and 2023, we interviewed more than 4,000 C-level executives across four separate surveys. We asked them about their consumption of thought leadership content and the influence it has on their business purchase decisions and investments. Perhaps most important, we asked: Does thought leadership deliver quantifiable business impact? For whom? And how much?

Half of the executives we surveyed were CEOs, who lead organizations with annual revenues of $29 billion or more. The remaining 50% comprised CFOs, CSCOs, CTOs, CIOs, and when it came to questions specifically about generative AI, CMOs. All-in-all, a representative sample of the world's most influential C-suite decision makers.

Whenever you see data represented in this book, unless otherwise indicated, it will be from one or more of these surveys. A detailed methodology can be found in the Appendix.

Results from the surveys and our analysis around them were astounding. Across industries and geographies, nearly all executives reported that the thought leadership they consume not only helps them make better business decisions, it also directly influences their buying decisions.

Beyond ROI, our research also found that thought leadership that includes original research, rigorous analysis, and subject matter expertise drives hundreds of billions in corporate spending annually. When it is viewed as independent of the producing organization's sales activity, there is a positive spillover effect: organizations that produce it are perceived as more trustworthy and are rewarded more of the overall spend than their more overtly commercial peers.

Even though thought leadership is often perceived as a cost center, our data shows thought leadership is, in fact, a revenue driver that is underappreciated, underutilized, and little understood in most organizations.

Why Thought Leadership – And Why Now?

Thought leadership is a critical tool for executives operating in uncharted territory. It lets business leaders explore problems without the bias inherent in internal brainstorms. It provides provocative, evidence-based insights. Building on primary research, external expertise, and practical examples, it delivers intelligence that helps leaders make smarter, faster business decisions.

Even so, until now, the real value of thought leadership has been elusive. Return on investment (ROI) calculations have been based on assumptions and leaps of faith rather than real-world data. That's partly because the world's largest thought leadership–producing organizations have traditionally been the world's largest strategy consultancies. Many have used thought leadership content to drive business growth for a century or more.

Partners in those firms are measured and rewarded on how much thought leadership they publish, so the consultancies produce thousands of reports each year, distributed to millions of readers. Consulting partners will tell you they don't care about calculating the ROI because thought leadership *IS* their business model.

They just know it works. The rest of us have to prove it. That's what this book aims to do.

The Wizardry of Evidence-Based Intelligence

The first written reference to thought leadership appeared in the 1876 Theistic Annual, which described Ralph Waldo Emerson as demonstrating the *"wizard power of a thought-leader."* Fast forward a century or so to 1994, and economist Joel Kurtzman, the founding editor of *Strategy+Business* magazine, is credited with resurfacing "thought leadership" and placing it in a modern context. He wrote, thought leaders "have distinctively original ideas, unique points of view, and new insights."[1]

Wizardry aside, we define thought leadership as distinctive, evidence-based intelligence that gives leaders the insights they need to make better business decisions. It builds trust and credibility – which may be why so many executives regularly spend time with thought leadership. Almost 9 in 10 (88%) executives say they spend about two hours each week consuming thought leadership.

Why are they so invested? Almost all (96%) business leaders who consume thought leadership say they make better decisions as a result. And those results inspire them to take action: 87% of executives say they made a specific purchase decision in the previous 90 days as a direct result of consuming thought leadership.

By our estimates, the cumulative value of purchases made directly as a result of executives consuming thought leadership is $265 billion each year globally, more than $100 billion in the United States.

Those are big numbers. We'll unpack them later. But first, we need to understand what thought leadership is and isn't, and its rightful role in an organization's marketing mix.

Why This Book?

Our groundbreaking research calculates the data-informed ROI of a thought leadership practice for the first time. Calculations are based on real data – survey-reported business results – not expectations or estimates. And the results are eye-opening.

Thought leadership delivers an ROI of 156%, which is 16 times more effective than typical marketing approaches.[2] We calculate that organizations around the globe purchase $265 billion in products and services annually as a result of executives consuming thought leadership. In the United States alone, the opportunity for thought leadership–producing organizations is upwards of $100 billion.

In this book, we will explore the specific calculations behind these figures, discuss how executives use thought leadership, and quantify the exponential value that comes from producing thought leadership that is trustworthy and independent of the organization's commercial activity. We will also share a ROI calculator that organizations can use to justify the value of thought leadership in budget negotiations.

Marketers take note: While the debate about thought leadership's role in marketing will rage on, the returns it produces – both long and short term – can't be ignored. Thought leadership is so crucial that you might think of it as the new 8th P of Marketing – the platform on which every other promotion should be built.

Why Us?

Who better to investigate the value of thought leadership than those who produce it for a living – those who do research every day and turn it into the insights that are used by executives to make business decisions impacting organizations and industries on a global scale . . . those who have spent a career using thought leadership to generate interest, engender loyalty, and build brands.

In this book, we turn the research lens on our own thought leadership discipline, to investigate and quantify the value of our chosen practice.

To do that, we conducted a series of anonymous, double-blind surveys. This means the respondents had no idea who was sponsoring the survey and we did not know who the individual respondents were or what organizations they were from. The 4,000 executives we surveyed spanned 16 countries and 20 industries (see study methodology in the Appendix). Answer options were randomized, meaning if two people sitting side-by-side were responding to the survey, the way their answer options were presented would be different. As such, bias was mitigated. To supplement that research, we conducted a targeted examination of the impact of generative AI, surveying an additional 300 US-based executives about thought leadership that is produced using generative AI.

This book proves the value of thought leadership for producing organizations and serves as a "how-to" for those who want to claim their share of the global $265 billion opportunity ($100 billion in the United States) by creating and sustaining a world-class thought leadership program that delivers proven, quantifiable business value.

Thought Leadership as the 8th P of the Marketing Mix

Modern marketers routinely think of their work in seven categories:

- Product: The physical offering or service.
- Price: How much customers are willing to pay for the product or service.
- Place: Distribution channels, retail locations, online platforms, and logistics.
- Promotion: Advertising, sales promotions, public relations, social media marketing, and any other methods used to create awareness and generate interest in the offering.
- People: Human factors at play in marketing, typically around services.
- Process: Procedures, mechanisms, and flow of activities by which service is delivered.
- Physical evidence: The environment where service occurs.

For a comprehensive overview of the marketing mix, see the Wikipedia entry.[3]

Because of its immense and distinct value in anchoring the brand funnel, we are proposing that thought leadership as a *platform* (quite separate from the "promotions" listed above, which by its definition attracts interest in a particular product or service), becomes established as the 8th P of the marketing mix.

What Thought Leadership Isn't

Fake thought leadership is everywhere – especially now when any fledgling prompt engineer can use generative AI to create some content. So how can executives know what content they can trust? Identifying the genuine article starts with understanding what thought leadership is not:

- If the content has a commercial agenda, it's sales.
- If the content is created solely to generate leads, it's a different P of marketing.
- If it is content that reports what's happening in the world, it's news.
- If it's based on individual perspectives with no supporting data, it's opinion.
- If it concludes only that more research is needed, it's academic.
- If the content repeats others' ideas, often in the guise of offering new insights, it's just plain laziness – or at its worst: it is plagiarism.

Getting the definition right matters because – as our research has revealed – the best thought leadership has a measurable and material impact on those who consume it. To influence decisions and drive sales, it must be bias-free, trusted, supported by data, and clearly actionable. When it is, it's one of the best relationship-building investments any business can make.

Once the baseline rules have been met, thought leadership can take the form of an in-depth report, a slide deck, a data visualization, or a video clip. It can be delivered via earbuds or email. It can be created by an in-house team or through partnerships.

The key is understanding what role thought leadership should play. It's meant to be a sturdy platform – a store of trusted data and insights – that can launch businesses in the right direction. For marketing leaders who see thought leadership as a foundational tool for audience engagement, the revenue is there for the taking.

Part I

By the Numbers: How Thought Leadership Creates Value

Chapter 1

Thought Leadership Boosts Business Performance and Drives Spending

In the race to become smarter, faster, and more effective, thought leadership gives executives the inside track. In fact, senior executives in every industry we surveyed see thought leadership as a strategic lever they can pull to improve business performance.

Across the board, four out of five (80%) say that consuming thought leadership created quantitative value for their business. That value comes in many shapes and sizes. Here are five ways executives say thought leadership benefits their business:

- **Greater revenue growth and profitability:** Our analysis reveals that 46% of C-suite executives globally – and 39% in the United States – strongly believe that consuming thought leadership helps drive higher levels of revenue growth than would otherwise be possible. And more than half (57%) say the application of thought leadership insights significantly impacts the financial performance of their organization. We also found that businesses with the fastest rates of revenue growth were the most active in engaging with thought leadership. Looking to the bottom line, the benefits of thought leadership are even more noteworthy. Roughly three out of five (59%) global business leaders strongly believe that thought leadership helps drive higher levels of profitability for their business.

- **Sharper competitive edge:** Almost all (96%) business leaders globally say they make better business decisions as a result of consuming thought leadership. Roughly four out of five C-suite executives in the United States say their organizations are competitively better off as a direct result of applying lessons learned from thought leadership. For executives in other geographies, the impacts are even greater: 93% say thought leadership gives them a competitive advantage. Why? Because it provides insights into emerging trends, risks, and opportunities *before* disruption forces them to react.

- **Improved innovation and business agility:** Thought leadership gives organizations the upper hand in innovation. Expert analysis helps executives identify cutting-edge growth opportunities and offers the "how to" insights needed to respond quickly to new opportunities. More than half of global business leaders say innovation (58%) and business agility (52%) have been significantly improved as a result of thought leadership insights. This could be one reason 60% of executives encourage their teams to use thought leadership regularly.

- **More satisfied employees:** Business intelligence that's both trustworthy and thought-provoking can inspire teams to raise the bar – and offer a playbook to help them reach new heights. Perhaps that's why 41% of C-suite leaders see thought leadership as an effective tool for employee engagement. Beyond bolstering their skills and expertise, 46% believe consuming thought leadership boosts worker satisfaction.

- **Fewer knowledge gaps:** Executives turn to thought leadership for information they can't access elsewhere. Almost 9 in 10 (88%) executives globally – and 74% in the United States – say they use thought leadership to compensate for inadequate data and analysis within their organization. Even more (93%) say they turn to trusted thought leadership content to gain a deeper understanding of the business trends affecting their industry and markets. More than four out of five (84%) use it to identify technology trends and approaches that may directly impact the success of their organization.

Thought Leadership Paves the Executive Career Path

It's not just good for business; thought leadership also influences personal success. Four out of five executives globally – 81% in the United States – report that the deeper knowledge and insight they gain from consuming thought leadership has been, and continues to be, important in helping advance their career progression. They're also sharing what they learn. Almost all (99%) executives say they share thought leadership with their business networks at least once per month; 86% say they share thought leadership with their social networks every month.

How Thought Leadership Influences What Executives Buy

One of the trickiest areas to research has been: How does thought leadership impact ROI for organizations that produce it?

To answer that question, we first looked at whether executives use thought leadership to inform their purchasing decisions. The results were clear: producing high-quality thought leadership increases the likelihood that executives will buy products or services from an organization.

For starters, 82% of executives say they're more likely to want to meet with an organization that produces thought leadership. Three out of four say thought leadership makes them more likely to buy products and services from that organization.

Among C-suite executives in the United States, 58% say they are likely or extremely likely to make purchase decisions as a direct consequence of consuming thought leadership content. As many as 70% of leaders in other geographies say they are either likely or extremely likely to translate thought leadership analysis and insight into direct purchasing decisions.

When we asked executives to indicate whether they *had* made a purchase decision in the previous 12 months as a direct result of thought leadership, 100% of respondents – across the United States and globally – said yes. That's not a mistake. Every single executive we surveyed said they *had already* made a purchase decision based on thought leadership – even those who said they were unlikely to do so.

We also found that most executives are influenced by thought leadership on a regular basis. Globally, 85% of

C-suite leaders (87% in the United States) said they made a purchase decision as a direct consequence of consuming thought leadership within the previous quarter. Of those executives, 37% in the United States and 29% globally said they had done so in the last month.

As executives grow immune to many traditional marketing tactics, thought leadership serves as an open invitation to connect. It demonstrates expertise and offers reliable solutions to real-world problems. Rather than pushing readers through a conversion funnel, it pulls them into a more meaningful relationship based on trust.

Our research has proven that this approach influences purchases – but at what level? How much money is on the table – and what are organizations buying? To see the full picture, we had to layer the results of our survey atop the real-world business landscape. The image that emerged is astounding.

Thought Leadership Drives $265 Billion in Spending Each Year Globally

The size of the thought leadership opportunity should capture every marketer's attention. Our research has revealed that billions of dollars are in play—$265 billion *a year* to be exact.

How did we calculate this number? We started by asking executives to report their organizations' revenue, as well as the percentage they spend each year as a direct result of consuming thought leadership. When we average that spending across industry, geography, and organization size, a typical business spends 0.56% of its total annual revenue as a result of executives consuming thought leadership.

If we aggregate annual corporate revenue across the Forbes Global 2000 – a total of $47.6 trillion in 2022 – and multiply that figure by the average portion of revenue spent as a result of thought leadership (0.56%), we get a global opportunity of $265 billion each year. This is more than the annual GDP of New Zealand.

Figure 1.1 Global thought leadership opportunity.

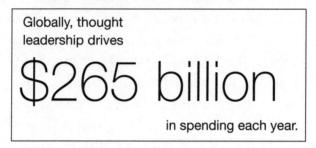

Globally, thought leadership drives

$265 billion

in spending each year.

We can also break this number down by industry and sector. Across the United States, businesses spend $102 billion based on consumption of thought leadership each year. And in the IT industry, organizations spend $99 billion.

This is just the spending that business leaders attribute directly to the thought leadership they consume. In fact, when we calculate purchases that are indirectly influenced by thought leadership, the impact grows even larger.

Thought Leadership-Influenced Spending *Around the World Is an Additional $106 Billion*

How much does thought leadership influence organizational spending decisions indirectly? Influence is difficult to measure – but not impossible. To get a clearer picture of the impact, we focused on IT budgets, where we have more exact data to analyze.

The global organizations we surveyed report average revenue of $14 billion, and executives say they spend roughly 4.7% of these revenues on IT. That means the average organization has an IT budget of $669 million. Global executives also say 35% of purchasing decisions are influenced by thought leadership – translating to a $234 million opportunity in IT in the average global business.

If you apply the same parameters to the average revenue of the Forbes Global 2000, the total thought leadership impact is eye-popping. Assuming thought leadership can influence 35% of $2.2 trillion in cumulative IT budgets (4.7% of $47.6 trillion) – we find that thought leadership influences roughly $783 billion worth of purchases each year.

And that's just in IT! Now we can use these numbers to calculate the size of the overall influenced opportunity. We know that the average global organization spends $78 million as a direct result of thought leadership – and that 37% of that spend is related to IT. If we assume the influenced spend has a similar split, then $783 billion is just 37% of the total. That means the full opportunity comes to $2.1 trillion.

Of course, thought leadership is just one of many external factors that influence executive decision making. So we wanted to go a step further and pin a hard number on the value of the contribution thought leadership delivers. Just as athletes are given credit for an "assist" – a pass that leads to a goal – we can quantify what portion of that $2.1 trillion spend can be attributed to thought leadership.

Most organizations have developed their own secret sauce for measuring these assists: proprietary models that calculate attribution, or how large a role specific marketing efforts play in a sale. Based on several decades of experience and conversations with our colleagues over time, we apply an assist factor of 5% to the total influenced spend. When we apply this factor to the $2.1 trillion in influenced spend discussed above, we can anticipate another $106 billion in thought leadership–inspired purchases.

That means the total global opportunity, based on purchase decisions made as a *direct* result of thought leadership ($265 billion) AND *influenced* by thought leadership ($106 billion), is a whopping $371 billion per year. For marketing leaders and thought leadership producers with a global footprint, there's arguably no better investment than distinctive, high-quality thought leadership.

Figure 1.2 Thought leadership influences billions in corporate spending.

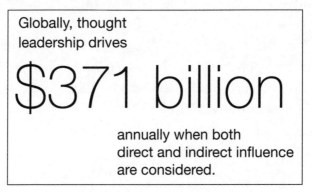

Globally, thought
leadership drives

$371 billion

annually when both
direct and indirect influence
are considered.

A Case in Point: Thought Leadership Spending in the United States

It's difficult to think of numbers these large in the abstract. Out of context, they lose their meaning.

To crystalize the business case for thought leadership, let's break down what the thought leadership-related spend would look like for a representative organization in the United States. Based on our survey's results, this organization's annual revenue is $29 billion – and it spends $184 million as a direct result of thought leadership each year. Of that $184 million, 46% – $85 million – is spent on IT software, infrastructure, or services.

Figure 1.3 Spend in one organization as a direct result of thought leadership.

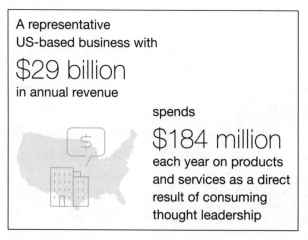

A representative
US-based business with

$29 billion
in annual revenue

spends

$184 million
each year on products and services as a direct result of consuming thought leadership

In addition to the $184 million spent as a *direct* result of thought leadership, 30% (vs. 35% globally) of purchases made by our representative US business were *influenced* by thought leadership. How does this add to the equation? Let's start with IT spend.

US executives told us they spend an average of 5% of their overall annual enterprise revenue on technology (compared to 4.7% globally). So, for our $29 billion average US business, the IT budget is about $1.45 billion.

Because thought leadership influences 30% of this spend, that equates to a $435 million opportunity. (That's in addition to the $85 million in IT spend that's driven directly.)

> *Thought leadership drives $85 million in IT spending – and influences an additional $435 million – in the average US business each year.*

Since the executives we surveyed told us that 46% of the spend directly influenced by thought leadership is related to IT, we can assume a similar distribution for the influenced spend. That allows us to calculate that an additional $511 million in spend is influenced in other parts of the business – for a total of $946 million. This nearly billion-dollar spend, for a typical $29-billion organization, represents the products and services purchased by our representative business because a leader was *influenced* by consuming thought leadership.

Applying our 5% assist factor to this $946 million figure, about $47 million is spent due to the influence of thought leadership. We already know that $184 million is spent directly as a result of thought leadership, so when we add the influenced spend, that means, overall, the average US organization spends $231 million each year because its executives consume thought leadership.

If we look at the US market overall ($16.1 trillion in 2022), the opportunity is massive. If US Fortune 500 companies spend 0.63% of revenue as a direct result of thought leadership – the average reported by the executives we surveyed – we see that there is a $102 billion opportunity for thought leadership producers every year.

Applying the same logic outlined above, we find that thought leadership also influences $526 billion annually. Using our 5% realization factor, we can expect an additional $26 billion to be spent due to the influence of thought leadership – increasing the size of the annual US opportunity to $128 billion.

What does all this mean for a thought leadership–producing organization? More on that in the next chapter, when we calculate the average ROI that comes from creating thought leadership. But first, we're going to dig one level deeper in our analysis of thought leadership impacted spending, by parsing the data according to business size, industry, and geography.

Figure 1.4 Direct and influenced spend in one organization as a result of thought leadership.

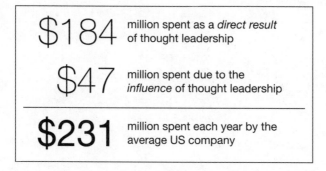

$184 million spent as a *direct result* of thought leadership

$47 million spent due to the *influence* of thought leadership

$231 million spent each year by the average US company

Three Factors Influence How Much a Business Spends

Though math might beg to differ, no organization is "average." Every organization is unique, and the spending that results from consuming thought leadership will inevitably vary.

Our research identified three characteristics that can substantially impact how much an organization spends as a consequence of its executives consuming thought leadership:

1. Business size.

2. Primary industry.

3. Operating region.

Business Size

It's not surprising that larger organizations spend more, in absolute terms. What is surprising is *how much* more they spend.

Figure 1.5 Larger US businesses spend more as a result of thought leadership.

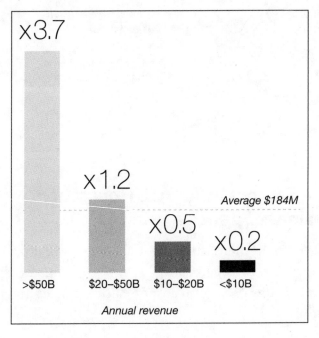

As you'll recall, an average US organization with $29 billion in annual revenue spends $184 million each year as a direct result of consuming thought leadership each year. But organizations with more than $50 billion in average revenue spend almost four times more than the average $29 billion business – an average of $681 million (see Figure 1.5).

Smaller organizations spend a lot less. When we look at US organizations that earn less than $10 billion in annual revenue, spending resulting from thought leadership drops to $37 million – only 20% of the $184 million average.

Primary Industry

Executives in some industries are more enthusiastic about acting on thought leadership than others. To isolate for industry, we drilled into sector data specifically in the United States. We found that organizations in the top three industries spend more than twice the average of $184 million each year (see Figure 1.6).

Executives who work for original equipment manufacturers (OEMs), such as Ford or General Motors, in the US automotive industry spend the most on products and services as a result of consuming thought leadership. They spend about 2.5 times the $184 million average, or $460 million each year. In contrast, automotive suppliers – the organizations that provide OEMs with parts – spend only $110 million.

Media and entertainment and IT executives also spend more than twice the US average – or roughly $405 million – as a result of consuming thought leadership. Financial markets executives spend $166 million, while executives in traditional banking spend $239 million. Transportation executives spend only 20% of the average ($37 million).

Figure 1.6 Automotive, media, and IT companies spend more than other US industries due to thought leadership.

Industry	Multiplier
Automotive OEMs	x2.5
Media & Entertainment	x2.2
Information Technology	x2.1
Government	x1.4
Banking	x1.3
Manufacturing	x1.1
Insurance	x1.1
Petroleum	x1.1
Telecommunications	x1.1
Financial Markets	x0.9
Healthcare Provider	x0.8
Healthcare Payer	x0.7
Utilities	x0.7
Electronics	x0.7
Retail & Consumer Products	x0.7
Life Sciences/Pharma	x0.6
Chemicals	x0.6
Automotive Suppliers	x0.6
Agriculture	x0.6
Transportation	x0.2
Education	x0.2

Average $184M

Geographic Location

Absolute spend only tells part of the story when comparing organizations from different countries. To level the scales, we also looked at how much companies spend as a percentage of average revenues (see Figure 1.7).

The average US business in our survey reports $29 billion in annual revenue and spends $184 million as a direct result of thought leadership – more than companies in any other country. They spend, on average, 0.63% of their revenue.

Figure 1.7 Organizations in India, the United States, and Germany spend the most on thought leadership as a percentage of revenue.

Dollars refers to average direct spend for each country resulting from thought leadership in a specific country. Percentage refers to direct spend as a proportion of average annual revenue of organizations in the sample for that specific country.

Japan
$68M/0.46%

S. Korea
$103M/0.44%

China
$103M/0.52%

Singapore
$51M/0.38%

India
$36M/0.68%

Australia
$34M/0.44%

Switzerland
$85M/0.56%

Germany
$85M/0.61%

Italy
$37M/0.38%

South Africa
$18M/0.31%

UK
$39M/0.47%

France
$91M/0.68%

Canada
$33M/0.44%

US
$184M/0.63%

Mexico
$22M/0.35%

Brazil
$41M/0.47%

Organizations in India spend an average of only $36 million each year as a result of thought leadership, which reflects 0.68% of their average revenues. This demonstrates a high degree of interest and willingness to act among Indian executives. In comparison, companies in South Korea spend an average of $103 million each year, which reflects only 0.44% of their average revenues, demonstrating perhaps less interest in thought leadership.

It's important to note that, even if the market in a specific country is smaller, the budget available in any single organization can still be substantial. For example, companies across South Africa are spending an average of $18 million each year as a result of thought leadership. That presents a sizable opportunity for organizations producing thought leadership in that region. The same holds true in other geographies.

Thought Leadership Serves as the Red Carpet Into Organizations

Investing in a strong thought leadership foundation has often required a leap of faith – or a marketing leader who previously worked with a big strategy consultancy. But through this research, we have been able to isolate and quantify how thought leadership motivates – directly and indirectly – product and service purchase decisions.

"Thought leadership serves as a red carpet into the C-suite. Thought leadership opens doors, builds credibility, and establishes brand authority, generating a return on investment of 156%, massively higher than any other marketing campaigns I've seen in my career."

Peter J. Korsten.
Partner and Vice President,
IBM Institute for Business Value

The evidence is clear for marketers. How business leaders feel about the thought leadership they consume strongly influences the way they feel about the organizations that produce it. When the thought leadership is credible, trusted, and seen as independent from commercial activities of an organization, the opportunity is massive for thought leadership producers. The only missing piece is a credible calculation of the return that can be expected from thought leadership investments. And that's what you'll find in the next chapter.

How Executives Prefer to Consume Their Thought Leadership

In our original study, we found that a typical business leader spent two hours each week consuming thought leadership. In later surveys, we saw this increase to just under three hours – a nearly 50% increase in just 18 months. They commit this substantial amount of time because they want to stay up to date with business and technology trends and learn how to operate and transform their business to drive revenue growth, profitability, innovation, and agility. Our data shows that global business leaders almost uniformly believe that they make better business decisions because of the thought leadership they consume.

Despite some commentators criticizing and dismissing the relevance of long-form text, our research reveals that a majority of business leaders – 61% in the United States and 68% in other geographies – continue to consume thought leadership in the form of traditional research reports.

Digital media, such as blogs and social content, also rank highly in executives' preferences. But they are rarely consumed at the expense of traditional white papers and research reports. Perhaps surprising to some, thought leadership communicated through PowerPoint presenta-tions ranks as the most preferred content form. As many as 62% of C-suite leaders in the United States and 72% in other countries reported that PowerPoint is the most com-pelling way to convey thought leadership.

Executives see a triumvirate of secret ingredients as essential to believable, compelling, and actionable thought leadership: original proprietary data, expert insight, and quantitative analysis. And when they trust the content they consume, business leaders are more than willing to share thought leadership content and insights with their person-al social and business networks. This, in turn, creates a virtuous cycle – expanding the reach of thought leader-ship while helping those that consume it make better, more successful business decisions.

Chapter 2

Producing Thought Leadership Delivers Clear ROI

Even ChatGPT knows that thought leadership is diffi-cult to produce.[1] It involves primary research, in-depth surveying, intensive analysis, and expert interviews – and that's before content creation even begins.

So, why should organizations consider producing thought leadership? Many business leaders might balk at the cost. But our research reveals that thought leadership isn't just a good investment – it can be a gold mine.

Organizations that invest in producing robust, rigorous, and relevant thought leadership see an average ROI of 156%. How does that compare to traditional marketing? Nielsen suggests that a typical marketing portfolio gener-ates approximately 9% ROI. That means thought leader-ship generates at least 16 times more return than a typical traditional marketing program – a massive and material difference[2] and yet more evidence that thought leadership deserves its place as the 8th P of marketing – the platform on which other marketing activities should be built.

As we explored in Chapter 1, and will further break down in subsequent chapters, ROI can fluctuate based on specific organization attributes, such as geography, size, and industry. It can also vary based on specific attrib-utes of the thought leadership that is produced, such as independence and trustworthiness. We'll investigate these further in the following chapters, using our data. In this chapter we will explain how we come to the average ROI figure of 156% – and you will notice that at each step along the way, we have actually been conservative in our calculations. This is, after all, the *average* ROI. Top thought leadership practitioners will return even more.

Figure 2.1   Thought leadership ROI.

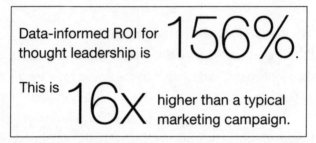

A Brief History of Marketing Measurement

Since P.T. Barnum and the Coca-Cola Company started using slogans and advertisements to promote their products in the nineteenth century, measuring the value of marketing has been a challenge.

The advent of digital marketing has made it possible to track customer responses to specific campaigns, giving marketers more insight into the types of activities that generate the most response. And yet, calculating specific ROI for marketing still vexes C-suite execs. The century-old quote attributed to retailer John Wanamaker still rings true: "Half my advertising spend is wasted; the trouble is, I don't know which half."

But half might be optimistic. Just before the digital marketing revolution, researchers Rex Briggs and Greg Stuart attempted to calculate the effectiveness of major marketing campaigns. They reviewed more than $1 billion of marketing spend across 30 major corporations and found an overall effectiveness rate of 37%.[3] Then there's Nielsen's 9% ROI estimate quoted earlier.[4] So there is clearly a gap in understanding the value of expensive marketing promotions.

When it comes to measuring the impact of individual thought leadership assets, marketing leaders might tell you they can track an asset's digital engagement, counting click and open rates, or they may track social media likes and shares. They might measure media impressions to assess demand – or gate their thought leadership content solely to gather leads (we'll talk about why this is a mistake in Chapter 9).

From these insights, marketing leaders may be able to tell how a specific asset performed compared to other assets or other marketing activities. To be sure, that's important information. But without credible proof of a significant return on investment, it's not going to satisfy a CFO for long or justify an increase in the marketing budget.

We've never met a CMO who could – or would – stand behind the ROI of their marketing program. Some of our colleagues tell us they measure success by whether their executive team is happy – and whether they're being barraged with questions from media outlets, collaborators – and even competitors – about what they're doing. They might use a motley collection of marketing stats to tell a believable story, but this is usually based on conjecture, assumptions, and comparisons. So, in effect, there's been no reliable way to prove the value of thought leadership as a marketing vehicle – until now.

Calculating the First-Ever Data-Informed ROI for Thought Leadership

Calculating ROI is relatively simple math. It requires only two variables:

- the cost of an activity;
- the financial benefit that results from the activity.

ROI is calculated by subtracting the investment from the return and then dividing by the investment. To get the ROI as a percentage, that number is then multiplied by 100. So, the formula looks like as shown in Figure 2.2.

Figure 2.2   How to calculate ROI.

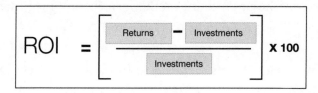

The math is simple, but measuring accurate and repeatable returns from a thought leadership practice is incredibly complex. To get to our ROI of 156%, let's walk through the model using a representative US organization as an example.

We'll start with how that organization spends on IT products and services, because as noted earlier, that is the area with the most complete and accessible data. As explained in Chapter 1, the average US company spends $85 million each year on IT products and services as a *direct* result of executives consuming thought leadership. It spends another $22 million due to the influence of thought leadership, for a total of $107 million (see the explanation of calculated influenced spend).

A $107 million opportunity that results from an organization's business leaders consuming thought leadership is, on its own, a significant and appealing lure for producing thought leadership. However, that figure alone doesn't quantify the specific ROI. Before proceeding, we need to think more deeply about how a typical $29 billion business spends its IT budget. It is highly unlikely that an organization would spend its IT budget – even if we are only looking at the proportion impacted by thought leadership – with a single supplier. It is much more probable that a tech executive would allocate their spend across multiple suppliers. We can use our survey insights to determine how this allocation impacts thought leadership ROI.

On average, executives in our survey say they consume thought leadership content produced by only five organizations. So, if attention is spread evenly, these five organizations will each get 20% of executive mindshare. However, it seems unlikely that executives will divide their time so methodically. They will play favorites – and not all thought leadership will rise to the top.

To calculate an achievable ROI for programs that are high quality – but not necessarily best-in-class – we applied a "mindshare factor" of 10% to the $107 million purchase opportunity. That means a thought leadership–producing organization should reliably anticipate about $10.7 million in revenue from an average client.

But to calculate returns, we need to look at profit, not just revenue. Because publicly available data indicates that a representative IT consultancy returns about 10% in annual profit, we used that number in our ROI calculation (see "Why Do We Assume a 10% Profit Margin?"). By applying this baseline to our research, we find that thought leadership produces, on average, $1.07 million in profit per client. Yes, this is a conservative number: just 1% of thought leadership–impacted spending. But let's see how it adds up across a business portfolio.

Why Do We Assume a 10% Profit Margin?

To gauge a realistic profit margin that would apply to our data, we looked at the annual reports of several major US technology consulting firms for financial year 2021/2022. Although there was some variation among businesses, we observed convergence toward an average profit margin of slightly more than 10%. To maintain simplicity, and adhering to our philosophy of using data-supported, yet conservative and justifiable numbers, we elected to use a 10% profit margin rate in our ROI calculation.

The Average Thought Leadership Practice Drives $64 Million in Profit to a Producing Organization Each Year

Now that we have calculated the expected profit from one client organization, we need to apply the return across the entire client base. Since we surveyed C-suite executives who consume thought leadership – not organizations that produce thought leadership – there is no data from our survey to apply. Instead, we looked at analyst reports and found that leading IT consulting firms typically have 200 key or priority clients.

Unfortunately, it's not realistic to believe that thought leadership will be stunningly effective across all of a company's top accounts. Therefore, to complete our return calculation, we need to determine what portion of the client portfolio a typical thought leadership practice influences.

Data from our survey suggests that a typical thought leadership producer successfully reaches around 30% of a random set of clients (see "Why Does Our Calculation Include 200 Clients With 30% Penetration?"). Your clients are not randomly selected, so your thought leadership penetration rate could be significantly higher.

Using these calculations, $1.07 million in profit is earned from each client reached. This tells us that the average organization sees $64 million in profit as a result of producing thought leadership each year. This is the "return" variable in our ROI calculation.

Figure 2.3   ROI calculation – profit parameter.

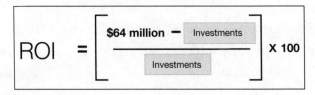

$$ROI = \left[\frac{\$64\ \text{million} - \text{Investments}}{\text{Investments}} \right] \times 100$$

Why Does Our Calculation Include 200 Clients With 30% Penetration?

To determine how many key accounts a major IT business manages, on average, we turned to Wall Street analyst reports. As most IT organizations are publicly traded and enthusiastic in positioning themselves as leaders in the IT industry, they typically engage with analysts to demonstrate their expertise, reliability, and resilience. Providing insight into client breadth is typically part of those analyst conversations and reports. Therefore, it was relatively easy to take a sample of major IT providers and establish 200 key accounts as a broadly representative number. To establish the 30% thought leadership penetration rate among clients, we looked to our survey results. We were able to establish that a typical piece of thought leadership was consumed by 30% of a randomly selected set of organizations.

How Much Organizations Spend on Producing Thought Leadership

But how much does producing thought leadership cost? As we mentioned earlier, it is not a task that can be undertaken lightly. Content must include original research, rigorous validation, and expert analysis – otherwise it is only thought *followership*.

Our research did not survey thought leadership–producing organizations, so to assess the investment of thought leadership, we turned to our own experience and professional networks. Based on our budget history – as well as conversations with colleagues at other large, influential thought leadership–producing organizations – we determined that average companies invest roughly $25 million annually in producing thought leadership (see "Why Does our Calculation Include a $25 Million Thought Leadership Budget?").

Of course, your organization's investment may differ. We'll demonstrate how to calculate your own thought leadership ROI later in Chapter 3, using the model and parameters we developed from the research. But for the purpose of calculating a defensible, reasonable thought leadership ROI, $25 million is sufficient.

Figure 2.4 ROI calculation – profit and investment parameters.

$$ROI = \left[\frac{\$64 \text{ million} - \$25 \text{ million}}{\$25 \text{ million}} \right] \times 100$$

In the final calculation, based on our survey data, a representative thought leadership–producing organization in the United States – with an average client portfolio and profitability rate – should reliably expect a return on investment of 156%.

Figure 2.5 ROI calculation.

$$156\% = \left[\frac{\$64 \text{ million} - \$25 \text{ million}}{\$25 \text{ million}} \right] \times 100$$

Why Does Our Calculation Include a $25 Million Thought Leadership Budget?

Thought leadership budgets can vary dramatically among organizations – ranging from tens of thousands to hundreds of millions of dollars. Indeed, some top thought leadership producers have a readership that is many times larger than leading business journals. How executives define thought leadership investments is another variable to consider.

Having spoken to dozens of thought leadership practitioners, we have concluded that, to achieve and sustain the impacts of thought leadership described in this book, an organization would need to invest around $25 million on thought leadership every year. Marketing and communications spending is not included in this estimate – that might be many times more than $25 million for a thought leadership producer of moderate size. For investment purposes, we are referring to spending directly related to producing thought leadership. This includes data gathering, statistical analysis, subject matter expertise, editorial production, design, and distribution.

Calculating a Maximum Hypothetical ROI, Just for Fun

It is unlikely that any thought leadership producer could capture every dollar of thought leadership–related spending from one consuming organization. However, based on our data, we can calculate the hypothetical maximum ROI generated by thought leadership, just to see what it looks like.

We saw earlier that, for a representative US business with $29 billion in annual revenue, business leaders spend $184 million each year as a direct result of consuming thought leadership. They spend an additional $47 million due to the influence of thought leadership. That comes to $231 million in total.

If we assume that an average thought leadership–producing organization can capitalize on 10% of this opportunity, on which there is a 10% profit margin, the $231 million becomes $2.31 million in profit per client. If we again assume 200 clients with a 30% penetration rate, we come up with overall profit of $138.6 million across the entire client base. If we assume the cost of producing thought leadership remains the same, ROI is calculated as $138.6 million minus $25 million divided by $25 million and then multiplied by 100, and we get ROI – perhaps not unlikely for the best performers – of 454%.

"We don't produce thought leadership because we're enamored with it; we invest in thought leadership because it drives quantifiable benefit to our organization."

"I remember an argument I had with our director of research, who wanted to keep our data secret – he thought sharing what we knew would give our competitors too much detail about our strategy for growth. But I convinced him to try using thought leadership as a competitive advantage, and built a thriving thought

(continued)

(continued)

leadership competency. We had amazing success based on a couple of anchor pieces.

One was our 'Pulse of the Profession' series, which featured the latest data on project success rates and reasons for failure. This insight was immensely valuable to our corporate and government partners and helped us demonstrate that formal project and program management were essential for successful strategy implementation. These reports routinely opened doors for our account teams to carry on conversations with operations chiefs about how to embed project management in strategy and operations most effectively, and they set the stage for PMI's eventual position as a driver of the project economy.

The second anchor piece was our salary survey, which demonstrated with data that people who maintained professional certifications were better compensated in similar jobs compared with those without certifications. This annual thought leadership survey helped validate the career decisions of the millions of certified professionals around the world who made the investment in their own professional growth by earning a certification.

Overall, our thought leadership program was instrumental in helping grow the organization 560% over my tenure at PMI."

Mark A. Langley
President & CEO (ret.),
The Project Management Institute

ROI From Thought Leadership Compared to ROI From More Traditional Marketing Campaigns

The long-standing struggle to quantify the value of thought leadership has made it highly vulnerable to organizational politics. Marketing leaders are often asked to produce thought leadership to support an upline executive's pet projects or in response to a "gut feel."

Lack of proof can make thought leadership portfolios prime candidates for budget cutting when belts are tightened. It leaves this essential marketing platform open to being corrupted, misunderstood, and misapplied. We have seen time and time again that thought leadership programs – even those that have been around for decades – are often only one leadership change away from being disbanded.

And *that,* our research found, creates a huge, missed opportunity.

It's rare that an organization can calculate and compare the ROI of specific elements within a marketing program – largely because many of the activities work in concert with each other. But every CMO or marketing leader now has the evidence they need to position thought leadership as an ideal platform to support a robust and effective marketing portfolio.

Chapter 3

Calculating Your Organization's Specific Thought Leadership ROI

Utilizing the parameters outlined in the previous chapter, we have created a practical tool you can use to calculate your own organization's thought leadership ROI. The parameters below reflect the average organization represented in our survey.

Figure 3.1 Thought leadership ROI calculation tool.

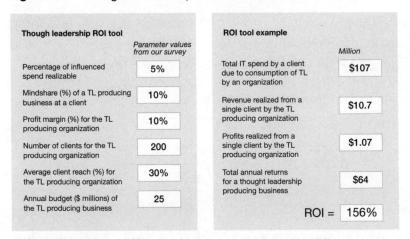

Though leadership ROI tool	Parameter values from our survey	ROI tool example	Million
Percentage of influenced spend realizable	5%	Total IT spend by a client due to consumption of TL by an organization	$107
Mindshare (%) of a TL producing business at a client	10%	Revenue realized from a single client by the TL producing organization	$10.7
Profit margin (%) for the TL producing organization	10%	Profits realized from a single client by the TL producing organization	$1.07
Number of clients for the TL producing organization	200		
Average client reach (%) for the TL producing organization	30%	Total annual returns for a thought leadership producing business	$64
Annual budget ($ millions) of the TL producing business	25	ROI =	156%

Your organization might have more or fewer clients or a different profit margin. Your thought leadership budget might not be $25 million. Whatever your specific situation, the model in Figure 3.1 allows you to adjust any or all of the parameters to calculate your organization's specific thought leadership ROI.

What if you don't have or can't get numbers specific to your own organization? In that case, the calculation we provide here is derived from authentic, independent, unbiased data. It is rigorous and defensible, and you can use it to justify your budget requests to achieve specific outcomes.

ROI Calculation Instructions

To calculate ROI, you need two things:

- Your organization's income resulting from thought leadership (how much revenue or profit you earn based on thought leadership)
- Your investment in thought leadership (how much you spend on producing thought leadership)

Once you have those two numbers, it's a very simple math problem. But like many things, the devil is in the detail. So let's break it down. Here's the formula again:

Figure 3.2 How to calculate ROI.

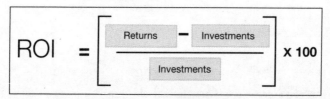

Calculating income resulting from thought leadership

Getting to thought leadership–generated income requires some calculation. You'll need to collect:

A. Total spend in a typical client organization as a result of consuming thought leadership = A1 + (A2*A3).

A1. Total spend in one client organization that is driven by thought leadership *directly*.

A2. Total spend in one client organization that is *indirectly influenced* by thought leadership.

A3. Percentage of influenced spend that is *realizable* by one producing organization.

B. Number of clients in your portfolio.

C. The mindshare your thought leadership commands within your client base (how many other thought leadership–producing organizations do you compete with and what share of client attention you have compared to them).

D. The reach of your thought leadership across the client portfolio (what percentage of your client base can you reach consistently and reliably).

E. Your organization's profit margin.

Most of us aren't going to have organization-specific numbers for all of these parameters, particularly the spend numbers. But don't panic. We collected these parameters in our global survey – so if you don't have them, you can use ours. In other words, where you have gaps, you can simply plug in the values we have calculated based on our global data.

To make it even easier, we have populated the ROI calculation model with our data in gray. For each item, write over them with your own numbers or use ours. It's your choice. Be assured, as we've demonstrated in Chapters 1 and 2, these numbers are derived from data (not random assumptions) and therefore are valid and reliable.

A – Total spend as a result of consuming thought leadership = Al + (A2 × A3)

Based on our survey data, when we look at IT-specific thought leadership–driven spending in one client organization with average revenue of $29 billion, it totals $520 million, including purchases that are either direct or influenced by thought leadership.

Here's how we arrived at that number:

A1. Amount of client spend that is driven by thought leadership *directly* = $85 million.

A2. Amount of client spend that is *indirectly influenced* by thought leadership = $435 million.

Total: $520 million.

But wait!

$520 million would be our final number *IF* we could reliably and consistently depend on all of this spend coming, in full, to one thought leadership–producing organization. However, we know that (unfortunately) it doesn't work like that, so we need to determine how much of that indirect spend is actually realizable.

In our example, **A3** = 5%. Here's why.

CMOs and those in consulting organizations are familiar with attribution models – which apply "credit" to the various different touch points that contribute to a purchase decision. These can range from 0 to about 25%. Based on a model we have used previously, we applied a marketing attribution factor of 5% to the influenced spend number to arrive at a total "realized" influenced spend of $22 million (calculation: $520 million × 0.05 = $22 million). If your organization uses a different attribution model to calculate realized spent, then apply it here for a more specific ROI.

Figure 3.3   Attribution percentage.

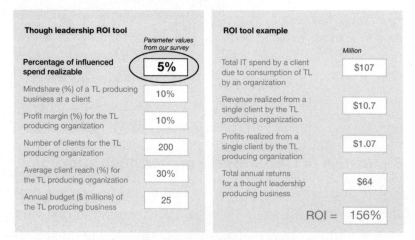

When we add $85 million (direct spend), and $22 million (realized influenced spend), we get $107 million in total spend from one client organization that is directly or indirectly driven by thought leadership.

That's your starting income number, unless, that is, you have a specific number from your own organization. We've never met anyone who has one of those! But you might be the first. If so, congratulations. If not, we've got you what you need!

Let's continue calculating our income number. We'll need to apply specific organization parameters to that income, such as number of clients, reach, and mindshare.

Figure 3.4   Total spend from one client organization.

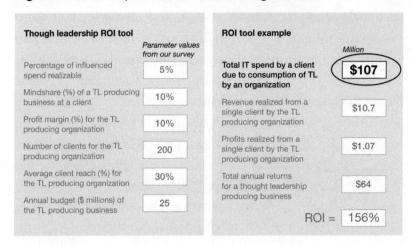

B – Number of clients in your organization's portfolio

If you don't know how many clients you have, it's probably easiest to ask your VP of sales. This number can vary widely and can have a major impact on your ROI calculation, so make this as accurate as possible.

Figure 3.5   Number of clients in your portfolio.

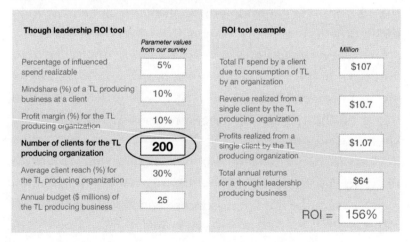

The ROI of Thought Leadership

In our example, we use 200 clients because that is a representative number of key clients that a typical large consulting enterprise has, based on analyst reports we've reviewed. If you don't have any idea how many clients your organization has and you can't ask sales, you can use 200 in order to establish a baseline, and when you determine a more accurate number, you can change the calculation to be more aligned with your own experience.

C – The reach of your thought leadership across the client portfolio (how many of your clients are you likely to penetrate with your thought leadership)

No thought leadership-producing organization could credibly say they are able to penetrate 100% of their client base with all of their brand messaging.

Figure 3.6 Reach of your thought leadership across your client portfolio.

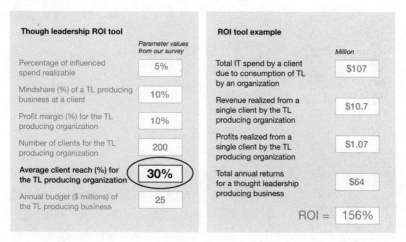

Though leadership ROI tool	Parameter values from our survey		ROI tool example	Million
Percentage of influenced spend realizable	5%		Total IT spend by a client due to consumption of TL by an organization	$107
Mindshare (%) of a TL producing business at a client	10%		Revenue realized from a single client by the TL producing organization	$10.7
Profit margin (%) for the TL producing organization	10%		Profits realized from a single client by the TL producing organization	$1.07
Number of clients for the TL producing organization	200			
Average client reach (%) for the TL producing organization	30%		Total annual returns for a thought leadership producing business	$64
Annual budget ($ millions) of the TL producing business	25		ROI =	156%

Based on data from our survey, we calculate that the average reach for the top five thought leadership organizations across all executives is 30%. That is, in a random sample of

Calculating Your Organization's Specific Thought Leadership ROI

organizations, a thought leadership producer in the top five is consumed by 30% of organizations. So, we apply this number to the organization's client base in our example. If you have a more specific reach percentage for your organization, based on survey data or other metrics, include it here for a more accurate ROI calculation.

D – The mindshare your thought leadership commands within your client base (how many other thought leadership–producing organizations do you compete with?)

Figure 3.7 Mindshare of your thought leadership across your client base.

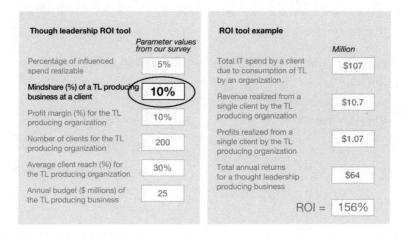

Business leaders consume thought leadership from multiple sources. Therefore, for each thought leadership–consuming organization, any particular thought leadership producer gets only a share of the total potential spend. Executives in our survey said they typically consume thought leadership from five organizations, which suggests a 20% mindshare for each of the five organizations. In our example, we decided to be more conservative and take that down to 10% to ensure no unintentional overinflation of the ROI calculation. If your organization has done research or you have another way of knowing what your specific mindshare is within your client base, use that number here for a more tailored, more accurate ROI calculation for your own organization.

E – Your organization's profit margin

Figure 3.8   Profit margin.

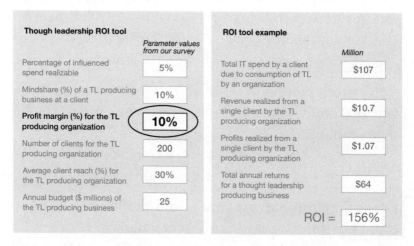

If your organization is publicly traded, you can find your organization's profit margin in your latest annual report, or in analyst reports. If your organization is private, you may need to ask your CFO. In our example, we use a 10% profit margin, which is an average profitability of the top IT consulting firms in the preceding quarter based on analyst reports we reviewed at the time of writing. You will have – and should use – the specific profit margin for your own organization, which you can include in the calculator for a more accurate ROI.

Calculating Income

Once you have all of those numbers, A through E in our model, you are able to calculate your thought leadership–derived income. Here's how.

To calculate income across your client portfolio derived as a consequence of your thought leadership, follow these steps:

Apply **mindshare** to calculate total realized revenue from one client organization	Total realized spend from one client × mindshare % $107 million × 0.10 = $10.7 million
Apply **profit margin** to calculate total profit from one client organization	Total realized spend from one client × profit margin % $10.7 million × 0.10 = $1.07 million
Extend the income **across your client portfolio** to calculate total revenue or profit derived from thought leadership	Total profit from one client × number of clients $1.07 million × 200 = $214 million
Apply the **reach factor** to determine return across the client base	Total income across client portfolio × reach $214 million × 0.30 = $64 million
This is the **INCOME number** for your ROI calculation	$64 million

Now we need to know how much you spend on the production of thought leadership to earn that income.

Identifying Investment

You will know, better than anyone else, what your organization spends on producing thought leadership. In our example, we used a number derived from conversations with colleagues in the industry. We found that leading consulting firms have annual thought leadership production budgets averaging $25 million. Populate this field with your own organization's thought leadership investment for the most accurate ROI calculation.

Figure 3.9 Investment in producing thought leadership.

Though leadership ROI tool	Parameter values from our survey		ROI tool example	Million
Percentage of influenced spend realizable	5%		Total IT spend by a client due to consumption of TL by an organization	$107
Mindshare (%) of a TL producing business at a client	10%		Revenue realized from a single client by the TL producing organization	$10.7
Profit margin (%) for the TL producing organization	10%		Profits realized from a single client by the TL producing organization	$1.07
Number of clients for the TL producing organization	200		Total annual returns for a thought leadership producing business	$64
Average client reach (%) for the TL producing organization	30%			
Annual budget ($ millions) of the TL producing business	25		ROI =	156%

Calculating ROI

At the start of this exercise, we identified two numbers needed to calculate thought leadership ROI:

- Your organization income (how much revenue or profit you earn based on thought leadership) – in our example, we know this number is $64 million.

- Your investment (how much you spend on producing thought leadership). In our example, we know that this number is $25 million.

Now that we have those numbers, calculating ROI is a simple math problem, and we can see the ROI on thought leadership for the average producing organization with average numbers of clients and typical returns is 156%.

Figure 3.10 ROI calculation.

$$156\% = \left[\frac{\$64\ \text{million} - \$25\ \text{million}}{\$25\ \text{million}} \right] \times 100$$

How does yours compare? We'd love to know!

Conclusion

With data that proves what we as thought leadership producers already knew intuitively, it is time to change the marketing conversation. We need to position thought leadership in its rightful place in the center of the marketing mix, as the 8th P of marketing – a solid and enduring platform on which to build other outreach and promotional activities.

Part II

Building a Valuable Thought Leadership Capability

Chapter 4

Rise Above the Fray: Creating Next-Level Thought Leadership

What makes your thought leadership better than something a prompt engineer could create using a generative AI tool? That is the $100 billion question.

A tidal wave of AI-generated content has leveled old assumptions about what differentiates information from insight. While expertise is still essential, a pithy point of view is no longer enough to set you apart.

If you ask a generative AI model, such as Chat GPT, to write an essay about how to solve a business problem, it can come up with some pretty convincing answers. And if you ask it to write the essay from the perspective of a specific type of solution provider, it can do that, too. The advice it gives may not be accurate, could be incredibly biased, and may be completely fabricated, but the content will likely be compelling – and take almost no time to produce.

To stand out among the crowd, thought leadership producers need to be strategic. They need to activate five value levers that promise a competitive edge – and deliver a purchase premium. Three can be completely controlled by the producing organization: quality, uniqueness, reach. Two can be influenced by producers but, in the end, are decided by users: independence and trust.

First, though, before we dig into the 3 + 2 formula, let's take a look at what generative AI has to offer thought leadership – and where it falls short.

Why Generative AI Can't Produce Thought Leadership (And Why It Shouldn't, Even If It Could)

Generative AI in this context refers to content that is produced from writing natural language prompts that query data that is housed in large language models. The output is AI-generated text, images, and other content based on the data the models were trained on. At a high level, generative tools draw on their training data to create a new output that mimics the original inputs using a "next best guess" methodology, tuned by prompts from hundreds of millions of users, uncountable bytes of data, and algorithms that operate in sometimes unknown ways, often referred to as a "black box." All this happens in just a few seconds, and the promise of increased productivity in the face of exploding demand has captured the attention of executives around the globe and across industries.

Information – content – is increasing exponentially, around the world and across multiple channels. Eighty-eight percent of customer experience and marketing professionals in a recent Adobe survey said that content demands at least doubled during the last two years. About two-thirds said they expect content demands to increase between 5 times and 20 times over the next two years.[1]

With this kind of pressure, executives may be eager to learn how computers could help them produce thought leadership more quickly and cost efficiently. Some may even be eyeing AI as a replacement for human content creators. But even the machines think that's a bad idea.

Here's what ChatGPT had to say to the prompt: "Why can't generative AI create thought leadership?"[2]

> Generative AI can produce text that appears to be thought leadership, but it lacks the ability to truly understand the concepts it is writing about.
>
> Thought leadership requires a deep understanding of a field, the ability to synthesize information from multiple sources, and the capacity to generate new and valuable insights. While generative AI is excellent at processing large amounts of data and identifying patterns, it lacks the creativity and intuition that humans possess. It is limited by the data it has been trained on and cannot generate truly original ideas or insights.
>
> Furthermore, thought leadership is not just about the output of ideas or insights, but also about the process of developing those ideas. It involves critical thinking, collaboration, and debate, which are all human activities that cannot be replicated by AI.
>
> In short, while generative AI can produce text that appears to be thought leadership, it lacks the true understanding and creativity required to generate genuine thought leadership.

The technology seems to know its limitations, even as executives interested in productivity improvements and cost cutting start looking to generative AI as a content producing machine. Content development is one of the

59

earliest use cases for organizations, who are leveraging AI's capabilities to recognize patterns out of massive amounts of data, simplify a complex description, condense overly verbose text, or adjust the tone and style of writing to match any circumstance. Even so, organizations that invest in building human-centered thought leadership capabilities with the creativity and critical thinking required to develop a credible point of view aligned with business priorities will be the most successful.

The Five Levers: What Makes Thought Leadership Best in Class

This 3 + 2 value equation provides a roadmap for producers of thought leadership to optimize their effectiveness. Thought leadership–producing organizations that major on one of the three primary levers over the others may actually have benefits over competitors who haven't found their niche or are struggling to hit the mark. Those that reach their target audience by producing high-quality content with a unique and compelling message can connect with clients to claim an outsize share of the market.

Our research shows that 95% of executives – essentially all business leaders – believe they make better business decisions when they consume thought leadership. And 93% believe that applying lessons learned gives their business a competitive edge. Those benefits are not abstract: 79% of executives say they can quantify the value delivered to the business due to thought leadership.

But *whose* thought leadership will they consume? And what will they find most useful and effective? While the opportunity for thought leadership producers to influence executives – and drive revenue growth – is enormous, the competition is fierce. More than 11,000 think tanks around the world play in the thought leadership arena. If each think tank publishes just one piece of thought leadership each month, that translates to 135,000 reports each year.[3]

We know that executives spend two hours each week consuming thought leadership – which means they must choose wisely. What would it take for an organization to become a client's go-to source?

It comes down to five value levers: quality, uniqueness, reach, independence, and trust. Quality, uniqueness, and reach can be directly controlled by each thought leadership–producing organization. Independence and trust can only be influenced. Thought leadership producers can move each lever by applying the right pressure – and generative AI increases the amount of pressure they can apply.

Quality: Establish a Foundation of Trust

If uniqueness is about the questions your thought leadership asks, quality is defined by the answers your thought leadership gives. Anyone can create an opinion about the business landscape – and now generative AI can spit out thousands of words per minute on any given topic.

In a time of instant analysis, thought leadership based on original data stands out. Our research demonstrates that business leaders who consume thought leadership look for expertise coupled with proprietary data and rigorous analysis. In fact, 65% of executives say proprietary data is important to conveying believable thought leadership.

Of course, conducting independent, double-blind research is expensive and time-consuming, which is why many organizations would prefer to skip it. Yet, as generative AI accelerates survey development and data analysis – and as synthetic data makes its way onto the scene, organizations that use original research to their advantage will take the lion's share of the $100 billion opportunity pie.

To be most effective, those producing thought leadership should be able to answer the following questions affirmatively:

- Is the point of view derived from credible research, which uses double blind/anonymous techniques to avoid any hint of bias?

- Can the analytical findings be translated into compelling insights?

- Are those insights provided as part of a narrative that offers actionable recommendations to address important business challenges?

- Who is authoring and are they a credible expert on the topic? Do they have a point of view that differentiates the content from similar pieces already in the market?

- Is the content free of any overt commercial messaging?

Uniqueness: Make the Message Memorable

In the age of generative AI that develops content at the touch of a button, uniqueness comes from asking the right questions and synthesizing the answers into new insight. If thought leadership is just rehashing old arguments without offering a new angle, it's likely to get lost in the shuffle.

As organizations tap generative AI to accelerate the process of creating thought leadership, they run the risk of watering down analysis and becoming part of the echo chamber. With the glut of thought leadership that is produced every year, those wishing to create an authoritative thought leadership program need a distinctive voice and point of view.

Executives that consume thought leadership are looking for credible expert opinions, with 82% saying these POVs are core to believable thought leadership. Similarly, 80% say financial analysis makes thought leadership more believable, and 72% say they look for economic analysis.

The message must be original, clear, actionable, and compelling. Align the steps you direct readers to take with your organization's business objectives and area of expertise – without compromising independence or crossing the line into traditional marketing or sales content.

Successful thought leadership producers will be able to answer "yes" to the following questions:

- Can you describe how the report aligns with your organization's business strategy and other thought leadership that has already been produced?

- Have you reviewed content already in the market that addresses your topic? Do you know how your report advances the narrative?

- Is the perspective different enough from other points of view that it will compel readers to engage?

- Can you produce multiple interesting pieces of thought leadership from a single survey? Can the narrative you are building be sustained over time?

- Does your organization's management team support the point of view presented by your thought leadership? Are executives willing and able to share this perspective with the media and with your clients?

- Does your organization have access to the design resources needed to produce thought leadership assets that are compelling, creative, and reusable?

- Are your organization's marketing, sales, and account teams trained in the art of building consultative relationships, where thought leadership can be used as a door opener?

Reach: Expand Impact Through Personalization and Alignment

Amplifying the "a-ha" uncovered by your research is the best way to expand your thought leadership reach. Here is where generative AI can be a terrific ally and tool for thought leadership organizations: It can deliver tailored content for specific clients or user segments in minutes – not days – which makes it easier to push out content before a hot topic goes cold.

Creating personalized thought leadership for high-value clients may have been impossible in the past. But now with appropriate use of generative AI, hyper-personalization may become a feasible strategy for bumping your content to the top of the pile.

Executives consume thought leadership from, on average, five organizations. That means a typical thought leadership –producing organization competes with four other organizations for an executive's time and attention. And any given piece of thought leadership is expected to reach about 30% of the organizations in a company client portfolio.

To improve the reach and expand the impact of the thought leadership portfolio, leaders should be able to answer the following questions affirmatively:

- Is your thought leadership integrated into marketing campaigns as the content engine, without being used as a sales tool or lead generator?
- Is thought leadership shared across your organization? Are executives, marketing and PR leaders, and account-facing teams given the enablement resources tools to understand, promote, and share the report directly with their clients and across their personal and business networks?
- Are your ecosystem partners aware of the content and prepared to share it through their channels?
- Do people across your organization accept that thought leadership helps grow client and customer relationships over time, even though it may not generate a lead or drive a sale in the short term?

Of course, the factors that an organization can control only take you so far. How users perceive your thought leadership plays an important role as well. To get the full bump that comes from being a credible source of information, your audience must see your thought leadership as independent and trustworthy.

The Independence Premium: Prove You Are Agenda-Free

Independent thought leadership is perceived to be free of any commercial or sales bias. By distinguishing thought leadership from sales and marketing material or corporate communications content, your organization can give your target audience the confidence that you have their best interests at heart. It shows that your goal is to help them get smarter – and helps build long-term, trusted client relationships that drive ROI without a direct call to action.

Our proprietary research reveals that globally, executives who view the thought leadership they consume as independent purchase roughly 145% more than those who don't. In the United States, independent thought leadership inspires executives to spend 74% more than thought leadership that isn't seen as independent.

Original data, objective analysis, and partnerships with independent associations all play a significant role in establishing the bona fides of a piece of thought leadership. And senior executives credit these independent sources of insight with having a 20% greater impact on revenue, a 27% greater impact on innovation, and a 21% greater impact on business and technology agility than executives consuming material more aligned with a sales play. In other words, the more credible the information, the greater its impact for both the organization that creates it and the organization that is influenced by it.

To ensure that thought leadership investments will be seen as independent, authors and producing organizations should consider the following questions:

- Is your research conducted by a credible firm, using a double-blind methodology that ensures anonymity and lack of bias?

- Could generative AI have introduced bias into the research at any stage of the process?

- Is the team or department that creates thought leadership – and the thought leadership content itself – independent of distortions or biases introduced by the business?

- Is the content planned and created without intent to generate a lead or sales opportunity?

- Does the content reflect an objective perspective (the market's view, with an analysis of solutions free of specific product references) rather than highlighting the organization's view, including liberal product references?

- Does the thought leadership solve a client or customer problem or offer a new way to think about a challenge?

- Is the thought leadership freely available to users outside the organization without commitment?

Trust: Build Allegiance – and Beware of Shortcuts

While a quick Google search will return hundreds – or hundreds of thousands – of results, and generative AI is now answering business questions like a trusted colleague at the next desk, reliable business intelligence can be hard to find. As a result, when discerning C-suite executives find a source they can trust, they stick with it.

Our study found that executives hold certain thought leadership producers in significantly higher regard than others. Trust is what sets these top-scoring organizations apart. By building a brand that differentiates itself over time, through consistency and reliability, these organizations have built a loyal following.

Executives believe the materials produced by trusted organizations are more likely to deliver reliable, vetted ideas that are distinctive – and based on rigorous and objective data and analysis. In the United States, executives who view the thought leadership they consume as trustworthy spend 110% more than those who consumed thought leadership they didn't see as trustworthy.

When asked to evaluate 24 of the most prolific producers of thought leadership globally, executives revealed a clear hierarchy in perceived quality. The most trusted thought leadership–producing organizations see a 115% purchase value premium compared to the least trusted organization.

Building a trusted thought leadership practice starts with ensuring your organization is positioned as a trusted messenger, meaning that you have the authority and credibility to be part of – or preferably lead – business conversations.

Our research tells us that C-suite executives look for original, proprietary data in thought leadership that is supported by credible economic and financial analysis. And they want that analysis to be delivered with an expert perspective. More than 66% of executives in the United States – and 82% of executives outside the United States – cite expert opinion as a key driver of believability in thought leadership.

Business or technical specialists who have in-depth knowledge of a specific technology or operational function can offer the expert perspectives that executives crave. In professional services firms, experts are often business or strategy consultants who have experience across many client organizations, industries, and geographies.

Professors or researchers can also offer expertise on topics related to their field of study, and many organizations have collaborative relationships with the academic institutions that employ these experts. Not-for-profit or professional associations can also be a great source of expertise. McKinsey, for example, co-publishes its Women in Leadership study with LeanIn, a charitable association founded by Sheryl Sandberg.[4] Partnering and co-publishing with these independent organizations can also give a company permission to speak to topics that may otherwise seem outside of its wheelhouse.

Experts could also be paid spokespeople, whether they're business owners, political leaders, celebrities, or activists. Increasingly, experts can even be social media influencers who have large followings and have carved out a niche for themselves. Organizations should be cautious about this approach, however, because if the paid spokesperson becomes embroiled in a controversy, there can be unintended consequences for your brand.

How an organization uses generative AI, as well as how AI models are trained, also has a major impact on trust. Audiences want to know that a real-world expert crafted the content they're consuming. They want to know the insights have come from reliable data, not the opinions people have shared online. In fact, roughly four in five executives say proprietary data contributes to the trustworthiness of thought leadership, while 96% say they trust content based on the reputation of the organization that produced it.

To create trustworthy thought leadership, authors and producing organizations should consider a few important questions:

69

- Are the insights provided based on credible, defensible research and proprietary data?

- Is the organization willing to engage in healthy debate about the findings presented in thought leadership content?

- Do the leaders who promote the content have the expertise necessary to explain and support the findings in public forums?

- Can the organization leverage partnerships with third parties, such as non-profits, to increase the trustworthiness of its content?

Follow the Leaders: Best-in-Class Thought Leadership in Action

It's easy to talk about best practices in the abstract, but what does excellent thought leadership look like in practice?

There are as many approaches to creating thought leadership as there are definitions, but as the practice matures, some organizations have been working toward developing consistent standards for producing organizations and individuals. Source Global Research, under the guidance of pioneer Fiona Czerniawska, has been a leader in this regard. Source is a UK-based analyst firm that has ranked thought leadership quality for the past decade and a half, based on four criteria:

- Differentiation – Is this piece of thought leadership relevant to me right now? Does it tell me something useful that I didn't know already?

- Appeal – Am I encouraged to read on? Is it easy and enjoyable to use?

- Resilience – Can I trust what I am being told? Do I know who is writing this and why I should believe them?

- Prompting action – Do I have a clear sense of what I ought to do now? Will a conversation with the firm be useful to me? (This last question generates debate among practitioners on how directly thought leadership should – or should not – serve as a specific lead-generation activity for producing organizations. We address this more deeply in Chapter 9 during our discussion of the role of a Strategy Squad.)

In mid-2024, the American Productivity & Quality Center (APQC), known as the world's foremost authority on benchmarking, best practices, process and performance improvement, and knowledge management, launched a Global Thought Leadership Institute (GTLI) as a "not-for-profit organization advocating for the standardized practice, production, and promotion of thought leadership. Through its network of world class thought leaders, researchers, marketers, editors, designers, influencers, and others, GTLI promotes the development of distinctive, evidence-based intelligence that gives business leaders the insights they need to make better decisions. The Institute serves as a strategic resource in thought leadership through:

- The development and issuance of standards.
- Furthering the profession through education and training programs.
- Connecting professionals at hosted events."[5]

Here are some top-ranked examples of high-quality thought leadership featured in the 2024 Source Global Rankings of Thought Leadership Quality, along with a few other standouts, from both large consultancies and smaller firms. These cases help ground our recommendations in the real world.[6]

1. Accenture

Title: *Strategy at the pace of technology: Reinventing business strategy to harness technology acceleration*[7]

Accenture is known for publishing clean, engaging, and dynamic content that consistently tops "must-read" lists. This report, ranked #1 in the 2024 Source Global Rankings of Thought Leadership Quality, offers a unique angle on a topic – business strategy – that is well covered in thought leadership. It is noted for its extensive research, clear methodology, and thorough analysis, along with strong audience engagement.

Title: *Electric vehicles on the rise*[8]

This paper differentiates itself by highlighting how noteworthy companies and markets are succeeding in an evolving automotive market, rather than just analyzing the electric vehicle trend at an industry level. It showcases specific business results these leaders have achieved and offers actionable advice outlining how traditional automakers should respond to change.

2. IBM Institute for Business Value

Title: *Women in leadership: Why perception outpaces the pipeline and what to do about it*[9]

Thought leadership takes many forms, and when a report can be leveraged across platforms, geographies, and time frames, it offers opportunity for derivatives and extender pieces. This report is a notable example. Its engaging landing page draws readers to the content while the robust research and analysis, combined with practical to-dos enable leaders to take action immediately after closing the report. The value and longevity of this bi-annual study have also been extended by the production of geographic derivatives, along with a related report that takes a deeper dive into one specific area of women in leadership: *Forging the future of AI: Women can take the lead.*[10] Co-branding with an affiliate organization like CHIEF is another notable feature of this report, which offers extensibility and opportunities for unique and far-reaching promotions.

Title: *Seven bets: It's time to bet on the future*[11]

The IBM Institute for Business Value regularly performs highly in the "appeal" category of the Source Global rankings, and this report is highlighted as a noteworthy example. A consistent customer experience that links the report and website landing page, an engaging video that introduces the seven topics, along with data visualizations and compelling case studies lead to impressive cross-platform user engagement.

Title: *Prosper in the cyber economy*[12]

The IBM Institute for Business Value is well known and respected for the depth of its proprietary data – this paper is a case in point. In partnership with Oxford Economics, the IBV interviewed more than 2,300 business, operations, technology, cyber risk, and cybersecurity experts across 18 industries and 28 countries to inform this comprehensive piece of thought leadership. It argues that cybersecurity is a revenue enabler, not a cost center – a perspective that is somewhat controversial. However, because IBM's Institute for Business Value makes the case using a wealth of primary and secondary data, as well as case study evidence, its thought-provoking analysis is both credible and trustworthy.

3. EY

Title: *When will climate disclosures start to impact decarbonization?*[13]

EY's Global Climate Risk Barometer differentiates itself by asking a provocative question – and answering it with market, sector, and financial data. It challenges current practices and preconceived notions related to the financial impact of climate change. It assesses the compliance landscape both locally and globally, building its argument by citing specific regulations and challenges companies face in each region. While the topic is complex and technical, the narrative is conversational, easy to follow, and creates a sense of urgency for the reader.

4. Bain & Company

Title: *Purpose-led brands can reshape the consumer goods industry if they can scale*[14]

Bain sets itself apart with digital content. While this paper hits many of the same marks as the other papers we've highlighted, it also comes with a more accessible digital experience. Of course, you can get this study in PDF format, but you can also easily scroll through the entire narrative online, including expandable figures and graphics. Bain's website also gives visitors the option to listen to the article, catering to the content consumption preferences of multiple audience segments.

5. McKinsey & Company

Title: *Investing in productivity growth*[15]

In the United States and many other major markets, McKinsey's thought leadership is consumed by C-suite executives more than any other. This study is an example of McKinsey's analytical capabilities and its intention to provide a big picture view while navigating a complex topic. It looks at the factors that drive productivity and offers a comprehensive guide for private and public decision makers on key aspects of productivity growth and reasons for changes over time. As with many McKinsey reports, the content engages readers with questions that might be asked at a business roundtable, making it feel familiar and relatable.

6. PA Consulting

Title: *Global threat assessment 2023*[16]

PA Consulting, formerly Personnel Administration, is a small, UK-based professional services firm. The firm is a member of the WeProtect Global Alliance, a network of governments and companies aiming to tackle online child exploitation and abuse, and in

75

that role produced the Global Threat Assessment 2023, highlighted as a standout report by the Source Global quality report. A key feature of this report, targeted to global policy makers, is its sensitive treatment of the topic of child sexual abuse – it manages to tread with caution when dealing with a triggering issue while also leading the conversation about how to create a safer environment for children. Including a glossary of terms and resources, this report is action oriented with a view toward the greater good.

Chapter 5

Eight Thought Leadership Archetypes

In Chapter 4, we outlined how activating three primary levers – quality, uniqueness, and reach – can generate immense business opportunity. For some organizations, however, pulling these levers can prove exceedingly difficult, especially when they are chasing quarterly revenue targets. So, we have created a set of archetypes to help organizations assess where their current philosophy places them in the market – and determine whether that's where they want to be.

Based on expertise in each of the three primary value dimensions, along with ability to scale and pivot, we have identified eight distinct archetypes that apply to thought leadership–producing organizations. It's important to remember that, unlike other development concepts, becoming better in thought leadership is not necessarily a continuous progression of maturity. That's because the three major dimensions of value – quality, uniqueness, and reach – are so distinct.

To capitalize on unique strengths, each thought leadership–producing organization should determine which archetype best aligns with its strategic objectives and then evolve the organization to enable excellence in that niche. This approach will best position them to capture a sizeable share of the $100 billion opportunity.

Let's start by exploring eight archetypes that can help thought leadership executives assess their own expertise in the areas of quality, uniqueness and reach – and find ways to improve in all of them. Relative strengths and weaknesses are identified by black rectangles that identify high expertise and gray rectangles that represent low expertise and the most opportunities for improvement.

The eight thought leadership producer archetypes are:
- Archetype 1: The Thought Leadership Novice.
- Archetype 2: The Thought Leadership Academic.
- Archetype 3: The Thought Leadership Narcissist.
- Archetype 4: The Thought Leadership Influencer.
- Archetype 5: The Thought Leadership Pioneer.
- Archetype 6: The Thought Leadership Nomad.
- Archetype 7: The Thought Leadership Pretender.
- Archetype 8: The Thought Leadership Superhero.

Archetype 1: The Thought Leadership Novice

Figure 5.1 The thought leadership novice.

The *Thought Leadership Novice* is just setting out on its thought leadership journey. Organization leaders may be convinced that producing thought leadership creates value, but they haven't built or acquired the skills needed to craft compelling stories that offer a unique point of view, so all skills are low and ripe for improvement.

The *Novice* may have started to craft a content strategy, but it has yet to fully align it with the business. Its thought leadership is built primarily on secondary reporting, as it hasn't established a credible research program. Building a following and media relationships is also on the to-do list.

Generative AI can help the *Novice* accelerate up its onramp. By streamlining essential tasks, from content planning to survey creation to promotional strategies, it can give a small team the power of an entire marketing department. The first step? Training your people to use generative AI responsibly, so that your thought leadership program produces content that is credible and trustworthy from the start.

Archetype 2: The Thought Leadership Academic

Figure 5.2 The thought leadership academic.

The *Thought Leadership Academic* excels in producing high-quality thought leadership content. This organization has deep expertise in gathering and analyzing data and developing narratives. But like research spearheaded by tenured faculty, the content is largely driven by the interests of an individual author. That means content is rarely fully aligned to the strategic objectives of the parent organization, which means the opportunities to expand promotion are limited.

The points of view highlighted in the *Academic's* content may or may not be unique, sustainable, or supporting any organizational goals. With the *Academic* archetype, there is little consideration for any connection to the distribution capability of the enterprise, either externally or internally. Therefore, the content is largely without audience, apart from the personal and professional networks of the author. Reach and uniqueness are low.

In short, the content might be extremely high quality, and it may be improving the eminence of the author, but whether it delivers substantial benefit to the enterprise is purely a matter of random chance. With limited reach and differentiation, it has minimal impact. The benefit of this approach is ease of implementation. When there's only one stakeholder – who functions as the sole author and distribution mechanism – thought leadership is easy to produce.

Organizations that want to move beyond *Academic* excellence to expand their impact should align their thought leadership content creation programs with their enterprise strategy. They should also secure commitment from the organization to use thought leadership as a door-opener in promotions, advertising, events, and media outreach. In addition, it's important to build relationships between the thought leadership–producing departments and the sales or account management teams. This places thought leadership where it can be most effectively used to build the brand and strengthen client relationships.

Generative AI can also help shake up the *Academic's* stodgy content ideation process. It can draw on search data to suggest topics and content types that authors haven't previously considered, and that are aligned with the organization's objectives, helping them make their expertise more relevant by discussing issues that are important to executives in the field, not just other academics.

Archetype 3: The Thought Leadership Narcissist

Figure 5.3   The thought leadership narcissist.

Quality	Uniqueness	Reach

Without expertise in either thought leadership content creation or market engagement, the *Narcissist* only looks inward. This type of organization creates content that is unique only in its self-promotion.

Thought leadership created by *Narcissist* organizations is often supported by management, which may mean senior executives had a hand in authoring the content. These pieces are enthusiastically deployed to sales and account teams to motivate customer or client engagement. But without the quality, substance, or authority needed to make thought leadership credible or compelling – and lacking the reach required to influence the market – too much of the $100 billion opportunity slips away.

The benefit of this approach is that internal stakeholders are often very supportive of thought leadership, which offers a solid foundation for a thought leadership program. But once organizations are ready to extend their external impact, they should increase credibility through robust research and data analysis and activate a promotion engine to boost engagement. Generative AI can make it easier to dip your toe in the water, but *Thought Leadership Narcissists* must focus on increasing independence and trust – not just pumping out content.

Archetype 4: The Thought Leadership Influencer

Figure 5.4 The thought leadership influencer.

Quality	Uniqueness	Reach

Unlike the *Academics* and the *Novices*, *Thought Leadership Influencers* are the darlings of social media – they've got a wide reach. This type of thought leadership organization operates as a marketing machine. *Influencers* know how to place thought leadership messaging in media stories and keynote speeches, and they leverage their ecosystem partners for added impact.

Influencers also have extensive internal networks and are skilled at infusing thought leadership messaging into the culture of the organization, enabling sales and account teams with compelling conversation starters. *Influencers* leverage every channel to their greatest advantage, and, as a result, brand recognition is high.

However, thought leadership produced by *Influencers* is often lacking in substance. Content may be low quality or duplicate points of view already in the market. Research may consist of inadequate or repurposed data with poor analysis, recycled or repeated perspectives, a weak narrative, and lackluster presentation. And because the content mimics what is being produced by others, it may be misaligned with the organization's strategic objectives. While this type of clickbait may attract eyeballs for a while, it won't help strengthen client relationships for the long term.

The benefit of this approach is that it is generally inexpensive, especially now that generative AI can do much of the content creation involved. *Influencers* who want to move toward a more authoritative and authentic thought leadership presence should build research and analysis capabilities that are aligned with strategy – and offer their own unique perspective rather than regurgitating ideas that worked for someone else.

Archetype 5: The Thought Leadership Pioneer

Figure 5.5 The thought leadership pioneer.

Similar to the academic, the *Thought Leadership Pioneer* has robust content development capabilities, as well as expertise in data collection, analysis, and storytelling. But unlike the academic, the pioneer is connected to the enterprise roadmap, creating content related to topics that are strategically aligned, with points of view that support the organization's position in the market.

Still, the critical aspect it lacks is market reach. The *Thought Leadership Pioneer's* marketing team doesn't use thought leadership as a content engine (whether the omission is purposeful or unintentional), and thought leadership

Eight Thought Leadership Archetypes

isn't fed into messaging for important organization-wide events There is little internal enablement, so neither sales teams, account representatives, nor ecosystem partners know that relevant thought leadership exists and therefore aren't being used to strengthen relationships and build customer loyalty. External media outlets are also unaware and unengaged, which means there's little media attention or social amplification.

The upside is that this archetype can craft powerful content that is strategically aligned – a capability that can be very difficult to build from scratch. Those in the *Pioneer* phase of thought leadership development need to move from alignment to reach by expanding their impact. They should consider building more robust promotion channels, both within and outside the organization.

Generative AI-enabled tools can supercharge this process by making it easier for potential users to query your thought leadership portfolio. Imagine if an executive could ask your organization's AI assistant for data and analysis relating to a specific business problem – the bespoke thought leadership it offers could attract new clients hungry for instant insights.

Archetype 6: The Thought Leadership Nomad

Figure 5.6 The thought leadership nomad.

Quality	Uniqueness	Reach

The *Thought Leadership Nomad* is both intelligent and popular – but lacks clear direction. This type of organization creates robust, high-quality thought leadership, and it knows how to distribute its thought leadership into the marketplace though media, events, and marketing.

However, the *Nomad's* thought leadership isn't connected to the parent organization's strategic objectives, which means internal sales and account management teams may have little interest in using it to build relationships with clients. Despite excellence in content capability and market reach, the thought leadership doesn't have staying power because there's no point of view consistent with the brand or goals of the enterprise.

With this approach, credible authors can continue to contribute their expertise and the marketing machine can continue to churn. But the return on thought leadership investment will be lower than it could be. As with the *Academic*, generative AI can help the *Nomad* test ways to refine the focus of its content. By outlining business goals and asking an AI assistant to suggest related topics, authors can get out of their own heads to see the bigger picture.

Archetype 7: The Thought Leadership Pretender

Figure 5.7 The thought leadership pretender.

Quality	Uniqueness	Reach

The *Thought Leadership Pretender* has a unique point of view that it distributes far and wide. However, under the surface, its arguments may be indefensible.

Thought leadership produced by *Pretenders* isn't supported by research or data. Still, its content may be enthusiastically supported by management and may be completely aligned with strategy. It is likely enabled by a robust promotions machine, widely distributed and quoted – but it won't stand up to scrutiny or offer the compelling conversation starters that come from thought leadership with depth.

Organizations that want to complement their shine with substance should build staying power with a research program that can provide evidence to support its point of view. Generative AI can assist in this area by suggesting survey questions and analyzing data as it comes in – cutting out hours of difficult work for your thought leadership team.

Archetype 8: The Thought Leadership Superhero

Figure 5.8   The thought leadership superhero.

Quality	Uniqueness	Reach

The *Thought Leadership Superhero* is the pinnacle of thought leadership. This organization has the skills and resources to create compelling thought leadership that is anchored in original research, data, and analysis. Its content is aligned with and integrated into the enterprise, while retaining credibility and avoiding commercial tendencies. Plus, the *Superhero's* thought leadership is powered by the full force of marketing, public relations, and events, as well as sales and account management teams, and a network of ecosystem partners.

Superheroes achieve an immense return on their investment from thought leadership, in addition to using it to build brand credibility and differentiation. Organizations that aim for superhero status should invest in the right talent and build expertise to scale content development and promotion. Understanding how generative AI will augment employees, rather than replace them, will be crucial.

An organization that can activate all three levers of thought leadership value – and scale its efforts with generative AI – is likely to be a leader in the field, with the potential to carve out a sizable chunk of the $100 billion thought leadership opportunity that is up for grabs.

Using the Thought Leadership Archetypes

While the eight thought leadership archetypes are useful to help leaders identify their program's strengths and weaknesses, it's unlikely that organizations will fall neatly into one category. Many organizations will align to multiple archetypes, and that's okay.

Thinking through these archetypes can help you break away from the day-to-day imperatives of content creation and ask smart questions about how your organization creates and deploys content. It can crystalize what changes are needed for the organization to capture more value from its thought leadership.

When an organization has established an effective thought leadership capability, it is likely that individuals from across the organization will see it as an opportunity or channel to demonstrate their own personal eminence and expand their career. And there's nothing inherently wrong with this. Publishing thought leadership can raise the profile of individual authors as well as the credibility of the producing organization. However, resources are inevitably scarce. Organizations are only capable of pushing so much compelling content through the production funnel. So eventually the question emerges: are you producing the right content with the right people?

Thought leadership organizations need to be mindful of the experience, role, and impact of the experts whose content they shepherd into the marketplace. After publishing a piece of thought leadership, the producing organization should be willing and able to substantiate, defend, and promote the content publicly.

If a piece of thought leadership resonates in the marketplace, it is likely that clients, business partners, or other stakeholders will ask for additional analysis and recommendations. And if the content is especially relevant, experts might be asked to present at conferences and other events – or discuss analysis and conclusions with representatives of the press. So, it's important therefore that experts have the gravitas and conviction needed to carry their message forward. And all would likely benefit from formal media training.

That is not to say that every thought leadership piece needs to be written by a superstar or senior executive. Often, major thought leadership content has multiple authors, encompassing at least some of the individuals that worked on the analysis. However, at least one author should be seen as an effective spokesperson for the content. While this person won't necessarily be positioned to make statements representing the perspective of the organization as whole, they will need to represent the content in a manner that aligns with the wider organization's priorities.

Control the Follow-Through

Imagine a situation in which your organization has successfully created a compelling piece of thought leadership content. There are several named authors of the piece, striking an effective balance of up-and-coming experts who are seeking to build their careers and more experienced experts who can represent your organization at events, conferences, and in the media to discuss the content in question.

What then? What happens if someone sitting in the audience of an event or conference approaches your organization's speaker and asks them to help solve a business problem or pursue an opportunity that was discussed?

While remaining distinct from marketing or corporate communications, effective thought leadership needs to provide a link to the products and services that the producing organization offers. To capture its share of the approximately $100 billion in purchases that can be attributed to thought leadership each year, content must tie back in some way to the producing organization's products or services.

It's clear from our research that the C-suite executives who consume thought leadership understand why thought leadership is created in the first place. They know the next step is for the producing organization to help them solve whatever problems the content discussed. That's why trust in thought leadership is so important – because executives know that future conversations will come with a price tag.

However, if the thought leadership analysis is overtly biased or self-serving, executives will feel less confident in its takeaways. Independence and trustworthy narratives are essential for business leaders to believe they are making sound decisions that are aligned to the strategic objectives of their organization.

To fulfill the promise of what thought leadership can deliver to your organization, the topics you cover must align with your business strategy. As you build your thought leadership portfolio, individuals will come to you time and time again with topics and research areas that have little or nothing to do with the objectives and interests of the business. While they may be fascinating and worthy of exploration in general, your organization should avoid such topics.

Thought leadership content must also remain separate and distinct from specific product and service offerings of the business. However, the most successful thought leadership establishes actions that a reader can take to advance their own business agenda – and those actions should effectively map to the product or service on-ramps of your business.

Most people don't like to be sold to. But, when set up properly, thought leadership can give experts the chance to master the follow-through: establishing the problem and solution, then turning the conversation to "how we can help." Clients consume thought leadership because they want to take the next step. But first they need trust in their guide.

Building a Thought Leadership Practice Through Partners

While thought leadership is typically branded by the producing organization, it is rarely produced without partners that provide expertise in specific areas.

For example, a consulting firm may wish to produce a report on the state of business transformation. That organization may have internal experts who can share their perspectives on the topic, but the organization may lack data gathering and analysis capabilities. To augment its subject matter expertise, the organization might contract with a third-party research firm to conduct a survey and analyze the data. Then the author puts pen to paper and drafts a report that is distributed under the producing organization's brand.

Similarly, a producing organization may be able to conduct research and analysis but lack the subject matter expertise needed to write a credible and authoritative report on a particular topic. In that instance, the organization might contract with a well-known author to write the study, which is distributed under the producing organization's brand. In some instances, an organization might contract with a ghostwriter to produce content for a named author within the organization's executive ranks.

Third-party partners can also promote thought leadership content. As discussed earlier, thought leadership is unlikely to yield value without effective deployment or engagement. For organizations that lack the capabilities or scale to deploy major pieces of thought leadership, contracting an individual or agency with content marketing expertise can be very powerful.

Whatever their strengths or weaknesses, organizations don't have to go it alone. Augmenting capabilities and building a team is a great way to become a *Thought Leadership Superhero*.

Chapter 6

Unlocking Value: What Moves the Needle

V alue is an abstract term. But the components that comprise it are not. Each factor that delivers value can be defined – and, as we learned, quantified.

In previous chapters, we saw that five value levers – quality, uniqueness, reach, independence, and trust, three that can be controlled and two that can be influenced – have an outsize impact: Thought leadership–producing organizations that activate all five levers win business, earn loyalty from their clients, and claim a larger share of the $100 billion thought leadership opportunity.

In our study, we quantified the value of reach – and this analysis offers a model for calculating impact on returns when even small improvements are made in thought-leadership execution. In this chapter we look at thought leadership value calculations through the lens of a sensitivity analysis.

A sensitivity analysis evaluates how changes in one or more input variables can impact the outcome of a model or system. It helps pinpoint which factors do the most to move the needle. By observing how outputs change when variables are altered, sensitivity analysis provides valuable insights into where thought-leadership producers should focus their efforts to see the most meaningful results.

In Chapter 1, we shared four key insights from our research:

1. Executives typically consume thought leadership from five producing organizations, meaning each has a 20% mindshare. We dropped this estimate to 10% in our ROI calculation, just to stay conservative.

2. An average piece of thought leadership is expected to reach about 30% of the executives in the producing organization's client companies.

3. A typical thought leadership producer (a large consulting organization) has 200 key clients.

4. 5% of the purchases influenced by thought leadership are realized.

To ensure consistency in the sensitivity analysis, let's assume that a thought-leadership-producing organization can improve each of these variables by 10%.

- 10% mindshare becomes 11%.
- 30% client consumption becomes 33%.
- 200 clients becomes 220 clients.
- And 5% realized influence becomes 5.5%.

In Figure 6.1 we've listed each of the four factors that influence the ROI of thought leadership. On the left side, you can see the research parameters that we used to calculate the ROI of 156% we outlined in Chapter 3. In the middle, we've highlighted how this ROI would change if each factor listed increased by 10% – and all other factors remained static. In the right-most column, we have estimated effort or difficulty levels for each of these factors. As you can see, moving the needle is never easy.

Figure 6.1 Relative sensitivity analysis of factors contributing to thought leadership ROI.

Factors contributing to ROI	Research parameter	Original ROI of thought leadership	Parameter with 10% improvement	New ROI of thought leadership	Percentage change in ROI	Difficulty estimate (H,M,L)
Direct mindshare	10%	156%	11%	179%	13.3%	Medium
Client reach	30%	156%	33%	184%	16.5%	Medium
Number of clients	200	156%	220	184%	16.5%	High
Realized influence	5%	156%	5.5%	164%	3.8%	Medium

Improving Client Reach and Penetration Are the Lowest-Hanging Fruit

The good news is that improving the rate of client consumption of thought leadership is the easiest lever to impact, with returns equivalent to the more difficult task of growing the client base.

Every thought leadership–producing organization has some kind of established channels to reach their clients or customers. Our data shows that almost 90% of business executives are regular consumers of thought leadership, so it is less a matter of convincing clients that thought leadership is useful, relevant, and important – and much more about convincing them of the value of *YOUR* organization's thought leadership specifically.

If your organization is an average thought leadership producer, similar to those in our study, your thought leadership penetrates about 30% of your client base. For purposes of this exercise, we are talking about increasing this penetration to 33%, which would increase the ROI of your thought leadership from 156% to 184%. That kind of impact warrants serious consideration!

In Chapter 10, we outline several ways that you can set about increasing collaboration with other parts of your business.

Improving Mindshare Increases ROI

Let's move to the next most impactful lever – mindshare. This is where you can see the value of using rigor to differentiate thought leadership in the minds of your audience. If you are genuinely able to increase the quality, uniqueness, and reach of your thought leadership, your organization can increase mindshare beyond 10%. This starts with targeting the right audience, meaning specific executives in key client organizations.

Producing thought leadership that addresses the interests and concerns of your most important clients makes them smarter and positions you as a more trusted business advisor. While our sensitivity analysis only assesses the impact of a 10% bump, you can potentially double the mindshare of your thought leadership by building personal relationships with this important audience. Our calculations show that doubling mindshare will increase the ROI of thought leadership to 360% or higher.

Increasing the Number of Key Clients Is a Heavy Lift

For any organization, growing the top client base by 10% is difficult proposition. Often requiring several years – and perhaps millions of dollars of investment in client outreach –

growing the core client base by even one key account might be considered a significant business achievement. This is not to suggest that growing top clients is not a good thing. Presumably, every business leader has this on a "to do" list. However, despite its lucrative increase in thought leadership ROI, producing organizations should prioritize improving other factors that are easier to influence.

Boosting Realized Influence Has the Lowest Impact

Even if your content shifts an executive's thinking, that doesn't mean it will inspire them to buy. Boosting realized influence – or the proportion of spend influenced by thought leadership that results in real dollars spent – has the lowest impact on ROI improvement. It is also extremely difficult to measure and equally as difficult to boost. So many elements comprise purchase decisions in business. Still, what is clear from the data is that thought leadership plays a significant role in purchase decisions. The more effectively you can deploy your thought leadership and improve the ways your clients engage with it, the more successful you will be.

What Does Sensitivity Analysis Reveal About Each Archetype?

The analysis above offers a high-level guide for prioritizing changes that can do the most to influence the ROI of thought leadership in general. But how can specific thought-leadership–producing organizations move the needle?

And how likely are they to achieve an improvement of 10% or more?

The answer depends on each organization's thought leadership capabilities. We looked at how these capabilities could take shape in Chapter 5 with our eight organizational archetypes.

There, we focused on the three distinct thought leadership value levers:

- Quality: Research, analysis, editorial and design skills and resources.

- Uniqueness: Distinct thought leadership POVs that align with business strategy.

- Reach: Marketing, public relations, account outreach, and events capabilities.

Figure 6.2 summarizes the quality, uniqueness, and reach for each of the archetypes, as outlined in Chapter 5.

Figure 6.2 Summary of thought leadership archetypes.

Thought leadership archetype		Thought leadership area		
Number	Name	Quality	Uniqueness	Reach
1	The Novice	Quality	Uniqueness	Reach
2	The Academic	**Quality**	Uniqueness	Reach
3	The Narcissist	Quality	**Uniqueness**	Reach
4	The Influencer	Quality	Uniqueness	**Reach**
5	The Pioneer	**Quality**	**Uniqueness**	Reach
6	The Nomad	**Quality**	Uniqueness	**Reach**
7	The Pretender	Quality	**Uniqueness**	**Reach**
8	The Superhero	**Quality**	**Uniqueness**	**Reach**

○ Low
● High

So how do the factors that influence ROI tie back to the thought leadership value levers? Let's start with mindshare. To increase thought leadership mindshare, you need to focus on *quality*, increasing the rigor and depth of your analysis and insight. Good content will find an audience. It all comes down to conducting robust research and analysis, creating compelling narratives, and delivering content in a compelling and sustainable way.

Boosting client consumption is all about extending *reach*. How can you get a greater proportion of your client base to consume and engage with the thought leadership you create? First, it takes mobilizing account teams and relationship leaders to position content with clients. But it also requires collaborating with your organization's marketing, public relations, and event teams to ensure your thought leadership is embedded in campaigns and outreach, without having an overt commercial agenda.

To increase realized influence, thought leadership must be truly *unique*. It must deliver compelling business guidance that is unavailable from other sources. Your organization must become a go-to trusted business advisor – and the business problems your thought leadership addresses should be aligned with the solutions your organization produces.

Using this framework, we can connect the value levers each archetype majors in with the ROI-driving factors they can most easily influence. For example, we know that increasing mindshare is tied to thought leadership *quality*. Given that archetypes 2, 5, 6, and 8 rank highly for quality lever, they should find it easier to directly influence mindshare. With respect to *uniqueness*, archetypes 3, 5, 7, and 8 are strongest, which suggests they can more effectively boost realized influence. When looking at *reach*, archetypes 4, 6, 7, and 8 have expertise, so they may be able to more easily deepen their penetration within the company's existing client base.

For the *Academic*, the strategy is quite clear. The academic rates low in *uniqueness* and *reach* but high in *quality*, which means it should focus its limited time and resources on increasing mindshare. If your organization is a *Thought Leadership Academic*, work to become even more rigorous in the research and analysis underpinning your thought leadership content. Continue playing to your strengths and build upon your reputation for creating quality content to own a larger share of the $100 billion thought leadership opportunity.

The *Pioneer* rates high in both *quality* and *uniqueness*, but low in *reach*. On that basis, it could pursue dual strategies of expanding mindshare and increasing realized influence. However, a look at the numbers shows that a 10% increase in direct mindshare yields a 13.3% increase in thought leadership ROI, while a similar increase in realized influence yields only a 3.8% improvement in ROI. So, if time and resources are scarce, prioritize thought leadership rigor and quality.

The *Influencer* rates low in *quality* and *uniqueness*, but high in *reach*. These organizations should prioritize expanding the number of clients consuming their thought leadership – and the penetration of thought leadership in existing client engagements. Work more closely with account, marketing, and communications teams across the organization to stack your roster with more valuable client relationships.

The *Nomad* rates high in *quality* and *reach* but low in *uniqueness*. So those working within this type of organization should consider a dual strategy of expanding mindshare and consumption of thought leadership across the client base. Increasing client mindshare and consumption both promise to deliver significant increases in thought leadership ROIs, which means both strategies can be powerful. While boosting client base penetration may pay off marginally more than increasing mindshare, both strategies should be advanced to tap the full potential of the *Nomad's* thought leadership initiatives.

For the *Narcissist*, while *uniqueness* is rated highly, *quality* and *reach* are low. The narcissist's strategy is therefore quite simply: promote, promote, promote. While the rigor and alignment might be missing, this archetype can still try to get more of its thought leadership into more hands to deliver greater organizational value. If you work for this type of organization, engage even more closely with communications and marketing, as well as account teams and client relationship leaders.

The *Pretender* has low quality but high uniqueness and reach. That means they should prioritize improving content quality to build credibility and authority. As they are strengthening that content development muscle, they can continue to get their thought leadership in front of more and more clients to expand reach and gain mindshare, which will improve ROI.

The *Novice* lacks expertise across the board. This organization should first focus on building skills in quality, uniqueness, and reach before they tackle trying to choose one that will deliver added value.

And finally, the *Superhero*. This organization is simply good at everything. All it does is win. It can do anything it likes, pursuing expanded mindshare, increased client consumption, and greater realized influence as its leaders see fit. Pulling each lever promises to deliver significant gains. But where *should* a *Superhero* organization invest its time and resources? Our analysis reveals the answer. Because we know that increasing client consumption yields the greatest increase in ROI, a superhero should adopt a similar strategy as the *Nomad*. Focus on expanding mindshare and consumption in equal portion. Unlike the *Nomad*, however, the *Superhero* is also likely to earn easy wins by improving engagement with account, marketing, and communications that boost ROI.

Precision Matters

We have considered five levers, evaluating each one against a benefit/difficulty framework. Based on our computational analysis, expanding client consumption delivers the most benefit and, if we look at the math only, should be the number one priority for nearly every thought leadership–producing organization. But all thought leadership organizations were not born equal, and depending on your organization's thought leadership archetype, the best, most likely to succeed, and most impactful strategies differ significantly.

Part III

The Four Key Elements of Thought Leadership Execution

Chapter 7

Balancing Your Thought Leadership Portfolio

A thought leadership portfolio is a lot like an investment portfolio – it balances different types of assets to maximize the chance of successfully achieving a specific objective or outcome.

For a thought leadership portfolio, key performance indicators (KPIs) will almost certainly include an ROI calculation – use one specific to your program or our data-informed ROI calculation from Chapter 3 as the baseline for success and to measure improvement. To move the needle, you'll need to pull the levers identified in the previous chapter to improve quality, reach, or uniqueness. But how?

There are four key elements that define thought leadership execution: portfolio focus, storytelling excellence, operational approach, and target-audience engagement. The next four chapters will delve into each of these topics in turn. Here, we take on defining and optimizing a thought leadership portfolio.

Just as individuals manage their investment portfolios by balancing risks and financial returns, an organization should view its thought leadership portfolio through a similar lens. While financial portfolios are subject to the opportunities, risks, and vagaries of the market, thought leadership portfolios must account for what readers, customers, and the media will find compelling. Finding and staying in the sweet spot – where your organization's objectives align with the needs and wants of its audience – constitutes one of the most significant strategic challenges for thought leadership producers.

Consider Topic, Technique, and Type When Building Your Thought Leadership Portfolio

Finding your organization's thought leadership sweet spot starts with understanding what your audience is looking for. In the United States, for example, C-suite executives have clear preferences. Overall, 85% gravitate toward analysis and insights around business strategy while 76% are interested in technology strategy. US-based CEOs share similar interests, with 92% looking for insights related to business strategy and 77% interested in technology strategy.

For global executives, preferences flip a little. Technology insights take the top spot over business strategy, with 61% interested in this type of thought leadership. Half of global executives have a strong interest in understanding financial insights, while around 45% look for operations-based insights and analysis.

Global CEOs concur, with 62% looking for insights based on technology strategy, while 53% and 47% consume financial insights and operational insights, respectively. Additionally, 59% look for industry-specific analysis and insights, 40% look for insights based on benchmarking data and analysis, and 21% indicate strong interest in analysis on society-oriented topics, such as diversity and inclusion.

If you haven't done an audit of your thought leadership portfolio recently (or ever), the executive data above offers a good place to start. However, you should also ask yourself and your team the following questions:

- Does your content address significant, strategic business challenges? How much of your thought leadership is focused on business strategy?

- Does your content address the mature and emerging technologies that are impacting your clients' industries? How much of your thought leadership focuses on technology strategy?

- Does your content offer operational insights that are relevant to your clients' industries? How is benchmarking data presented in your analysis?

- Does your content address the financial challenges facing your clients? How much financial analysis is included in your thought leadership?

- How much of your content addresses societal topics, such as diversity and inclusion or sustainability?

When these key themes are combined with the three levers of thought leadership – quality, uniqueness, and reach – this provides a solid foundation that a thought leadership–producing organization can build on.

From there, the content portfolio should be categorized by type and topic. In general, the content your organization produces should fall into one of three topical categories:

- Timely
- Technical
- Timeless

Timely Content

Timely content addresses current events – the urgent and emergent issues that are facing your clients in real time. Timely content can advance the perception that your organization understands market forces and provide the immediate business insights clients need to succeed in an uncertain environment. The quicker this content gets into clients' hands, the better.

Topics in this category include global pandemics, geopolitical tension or conflict, social unrest, economic shocks, and other so-called "black swan" events, as well as discussions of disruptive technology, such as the generative AI, the metaverse, or quantum computing. Understanding these events, and their impact on your clients' business, requires your organization to conduct or access research, then analyze and produce thought leadership, on a very short timeline. Content should be produced in days or weeks, not months or years, to preserve its timeliness and relevance.

But developing thought leadership on a tight time frame only gets you halfway there. Succeeding with this type of content also depends on a meaningful distribution and promotion approach. Because timely content is tied to current events, these topics can often be connected to events. For example, McKinsey demonstrates this with a sustainability report titled "Delivering the Climate Technologies Needed for Net Zero,"[1] tied to Earth Day, which occurs every April.

Technical Content

Technical content should typically make up the largest share of any thought leadership program and portfolio.

It brings extensive data, insights, and analysis to a business challenge or some aspect of strategic transformation. In terms of the time horizon, this content looks out one to three years into the future.

Technical thought leadership takes a deep dive into core areas of interest, aligning with the specialties or capabilities of the thought leadership–producing business. It should highlight examples that show leaders how they can take action to solve a business problem and what techniques have been successful for other organizations. For example, a staffing or recruiting organization might conduct research on the changing patterns and preferences of prospective employees on working from home or returning to the office that's designed to help clients navigate a volatile and sensitive post-pandemic environment – positioning its own leaders as subject matter experts and trusted advisors.

When possible, technical content should also provide an overview of what the most successful organizations do, as long as those actions can be substantiated and validated by research. Insights that inform specific tactics and approaches can transform thought leadership into action leadership. This component is so important that Source Global Research,[2] a firm that evaluates thought leadership quality, identifies it as one of the four pillars it uses to measure and rank the quality of thought leadership. "Prompting action," as they call it, ensures that readers know what to do after consuming thought leadership. These pillars are explored further in Chapter 4.

Timeless Content

Timeless content identifies emerging trends or looks at existing trends in new ways. This content can have a time horizon of a few months or a few years but should assess a current situation in the context of past events and future projections. It can make predictions about what may come or serves as an index, providing an annual or regular assessment of the state of a given industry, technology, or market. This type of content is similar to a feature story in a newspaper or magazine – it's interesting no matter what else is happening, in contrast to timely content, which is equivalent to a breaking news story.

To differentiate timeless content, the producing organization needs a unique vision – and the creativity to make that vision meaningful to today's business leaders. It must present a bold, fresh perspective in a way that makes readers want to share it with others. While it should be informed by data and analysis, it needs to go beyond the basic findings to explore implications that aren't immediately obvious. Building on deep knowledge and expertise that exists within the organization, it moves into unknown territory in unexpected and exciting ways.

It might introduce a new approach to business decision or articulate the rippling impact of an emerging technology. It majors on what's new and can play a tremendously important role in alerting readers to the trends brewing behind the scenes, encouraging a first look at what may someday be routine.

Examples of this type of thought leadership can range from the iconic Edelman Trust Barometer,[3] which looks at the degree to which people, governments, and organizations are trusted each year, to the Brightline Initiative's People Manifesto,[4] which explores why aspirational strategies often fail. For organizations interested in looking at the extreme long term, they could tackle a big picture forecast, such as the UAE government's vision for the next 100 years, which includes the Mars 2117 project.[5]

Thought leadership producers will inevitably have different abilities and priorities when considering the various topics and content categories on the table. Producers should play to their strengths, delivering the types of thought leadership their audience expects. But, especially in volatile and competitive times, audiences are also looking for useful and relevant content that is thought-provoking and inspiring.

Portfolio Content Types

Serving up the right mix of content types, meaning how insights are shared with your audience, is the next step in designing a successful thought leadership portfolio.

While long-form content often gets a bad rap in the era of snackable, social storytelling, our research found that executives are still interested in deep dives. A significant majority of C-suite executives in the United States who consume thought leadership on a regular basis continue to read research reports of all types: 66% regularly read academic articles and analyst reports, 65% read market research reports and competitive analysis, and 61% read white papers. More than half (51%) of executives say they read business or thought leadership–related books, with only 5% indicating they read books on a mobile device.

That is not to say that digital content has not been embraced by the C-suite. In fact, it's quite the opposite. Despite an age profile that skews older than a typical digital native, three-quarters (75%) of executives say they regularly engage with thought leadership on social media through digital channels. Almost as many (73%) consume blog posts, while 78% regularly watch videos and 62% listen to podcasts.

For C-suite executives based outside the United States, content preferences differ somewhat. Almost 92% of executives say they read research reports or white papers, 83% read market research reports or competitive analysis, and 81% consume analyst reports. A higher percentage of global executives also consume thought leadership content digitally. Almost 9 in 10 (89%) of executives watch thought leadership videos, 78% engage through social media, and 67% listen to podcasts.

Despite constant pressure to produce shorter, more concise content, this data shows long-form storytelling is not dead. In fact, research-oriented, analytical content should be a key part of any well-balanced thought leadership portfolio. But, like everything else, it must support a comprehensive portfolio of content types that align with evolving audience preferences.

While long-form research reports are most effective at communicating business insights with the level of rigor and substance executives require, creating short-form derivative content can give studies longer legs. Infographics, videos, articles, blogs, podcasts, POV narratives, by-line articles, social posts, webinars, and interviews can all be created quickly based on one piece of long form thought leadership. While these content types are more easily digestible, they also retain the credibility of the full report, bubbling up the key insights that encourage executives to take a deeper dive.

Overall, 59% of business leaders say they like to consume thought leadership in the form of interactive digital experiences that let them engage with the data and content directly. Slightly fewer executives (54%) prefer to consume thought leadership in the form of interviews or panel discussions or graphical representations, which can bring abstract concepts to life. Interestingly, notwithstanding the expansion of podcasting, only 20% of executives like to consume thought leadership through audio channels or podcasts.

While there's no perfect mix that will work for every organization, leaders can take a strategic approach to strike the right balance. Continuously managing and monitoring the performance of thought leadership will help you assess whether the content your organizations produces is hitting the right mark – and delivering on your objectives.

Chapter 8

Mastering the Mechanics of Storytelling

This chapter breaks down the mechanics of crafting a powerful piece of thought leadership, from the catchy hook to the provocative conclusion.

The Science of Storytelling

Stories give our brains something to hold on to, both cognitively and emotionally.[1] While most forms of communication trigger the regions of our brain that control language processing and decoding, stories go further, firing off synapses in other parts of our brain, including those that govern our responses to sensory stimuli.[2]

Stories also have more sticking power. They lodge themselves into our memories longer than isolated facts. That's because our brains treat stories as experiences – regardless of whether we experienced them firsthand.[3] It's all part of our survival instinct – the stories we hear could contain crucial details that help us avoid threats and stay alive.

The more vivid the details, the more actively our brains respond. A description of the aroma of espresso, for instance, activates the sensory cortex. A story about wrestling with a rusty lug nut while fixing a flat tire, on the other hand, might engage the motor cortex. The more areas of the brain sparked by a story, the more memorable it is likely to be.

While storytelling should be at the heart of thought leadership, it falls outside of the traditional narrative genres. As we have illustrated throughout these pages, trusted thought leadership needs to be anchored by credible research data and analysis and include a unique and actionable point of view – something that separates thought leadership from the typical "hero's journey," or "love story," narratives that capture hearts and minds. The job of a thought leadership content producer is to successfully bridge the gap.

First, find the unique themes buried in your data – then decide how to tell your tale. The most compelling pieces of thought leadership use facts like breadcrumbs, dropping them along the way to help the audience follow the story. Rather than throwing data at the wall and letting the audience decide what sticks, stories put the data in a clear context.

Stories make thought leadership easier to understand and remember, because they give people a reason to care. They're also more fun to read or watch or listen to – which prompts people to push through to the end, rather than turning away for something more stimulating. Plus, there's a payoff at the end – a lesson that inspires the audience to act.

Neuroscientists haven't yet had the opportunity to evaluate the human brain's reaction to stories that are written by generative AI rather than human storytellers, but whether the content is drafted by a prompt engineer using a keyboard or a writer with a pen and paper, thought leadership stories are a unique category with specific characteristics, namely an expert point of view wrapped in supporting data.

Even in this unique category, not all stories have the same impact. Here's how to tell a good one.

Tip 1: To Attract a Big Audience, Write for a Small One

Most authors have a sense of who they're trying to write for and what they want their research to reveal. That's good, but there's a trap thought leadership producers must avoid – trying to be everything to everyone with a single piece of content.

For instance, we'll often hear that a piece is intended for "CXOs" and "senior business executives." We understand this instinct. Given the time and resources required to produce thought leadership – and the business need to make a big splash – many authors try to make their piece relevant to as many potential clients as possible. In this vein, tailoring content to the C-level feels specific, but not restrictively so.

But there's danger in casting such a wide net. When a piece tries to be everything to everyone, it often misses the mark entirely, and that's especially true as generative AI enables the creation of hyper-personalized content that addresses one individual business leader's challenges differently than another's.

The C-suite readership covers many different experience sets, not to mention industries, geographies, responsibilities, and business life cycle stages. And however exciting research is, the delivery can smack of, "let me tell you what I know" rather than, "here's something that can help you solve a business problem."

Even without using generative AI, a better approach is to think big but write small – pick a specific set of personas with high-value needs. Senior business executives are busy, but also clever and interested in what's new. If the topic is compelling enough, they'll read on.

Much like customer segmentation analysis, crafting personas can help authors focus on the day-to-day experiences of their audiences. By identifying the unmet needs and addressing unanswered questions of a specific group of leaders, thought leadership authors can better address specific pain points in the format the audience prefers.

Broadly speaking, thought leadership content falls into the following categories:

- *Explainer pieces* seek to unpack a complex or emerging topic – such as a primer on digital currencies.

- *Issue pieces* present insights on a cross-cutting business issue – such as diversity in the workplace or corporate responsibility and sustainability practices.

- *How-to pieces* help readers learn the best way to approach a problem – such as "How to be a better boss" or "Five ways to buttress your organization's cyber defenses."

- *Persuasive pieces* make a reasoned argument for approaching a problem or idea in a particular way. Think: "Here's why your business is approaching e-commerce all wrong" or "It's time to reinvent the traditional strategic planning model."

Some topics lend themselves to more than one avenue of exploration, allowing authors to produce multiple pieces of thought leadership from the same body of work or to combine two or more approaches in one piece. This gives authors the opportunity to reach more than one audience over time or use multiple approaches to appeal to a single audience. Mapping audiences to messages at the beginning of the writing process helps ensure clarity – and avoid rework later.

Tip 2: Draft Your Thesis Statement Before You Dig Too Deep

The thesis is the "aha" message you want your thought leadership to convey. Like an elevator pitch or a killer X post (formerly known as a Tweet), it gets to the heart of your story and expresses the premise in a simple, elegant, and memorable way.

This is harder than it might seem. Authors will often ask to meet with us to discuss their ideas for a piece of content. In a 30-minute conversation, they'll describe what they hope to write about, highlighting the research, observations, and insights they hope to explore. Sometimes, they'll share an outline or even a rough draft. It's usually a lively and enjoyable conversation.

But often, authors stop short when we ask them seemingly simple questions: Why will anyone care enough to read this through to the end? What unique problem does your content solve?" "If you had only two minutes to explain why your piece is worth our attention, what would you say?"

While these questions can be annoying, that's not our intent. We know that our colleagues are intelligent and do good work. But we have also learned that it's often easier to just start writing than it is nail down *what* we're writing and *why* it matters for the intended audience.

This is where the thesis exercise comes into play. The goal is to create an idea that is fresh, takes the audience to a new place, teases out root causes, and offers a sense of what's to come. For example, suppose a research team conducted a survey that revealed women remain under-represented in the workforce. A basic thesis statement could be, "The gender gap persists." While true, that's not especially breathtaking. A report built around this idea would capture a "known known," since diversity issues have been widely covered. (*See sidebar: Scan the market.*)

Scan the market

There can be so much pressure on organizations and author teams to "get going" on a piece of thought leadership, that basic due diligence can fly out the window. This includes finding out what if anything is currently being written on the topic. Authors should do a thorough scan and see how the topic they're exploring has been covered, and by whom, and the caliber of research used. Secondary research, for instance, tends to surface "known knowns" more often than primary research.

Yours doesn't have to be the first piece of writing on the topic. What you're trying to understand is the degree of saturation and the approaches others have taken on the issues that you hope to address. Scanning the landscape allows authors to discern what areas others are and are not discussing – and how well or poorly. That examination can surface fresh avenues to differentiate your piece.

To take a more unique tack, the authors might choose to focus on a less obvious finding. With a twist or two, they could revise the thesis to say, "The more companies are spending to close the gender gap, the wider the gap seems to grow."

That's a more arresting statement, but it still leaves you wondering, "so what?" To be effective, a thesis statement should highlight not only the key research finding, but also what could turn the tide. In this vein, our final thesis might read: "The gender gap in the workplace continues to grow because organizations are spending on what's easy instead of making difficult, but necessary changes – reshaping organizational culture and mindsets," as in the 2023 Women in Leadership study from the IBM Institute for Business Value.[4]

Building a report around this thesis will require authors to explore the topic from different dimensions, going beyond mere opinion or basic descriptions of the current state to interrogate root cause issues and showcase true thought leadership.

This is the value of the thesis exercise. It forces authors to see if their premise can stand on its own, without being propped up by or buried deep within pages of text. Holding the thesis up to the light of day lets authors see where the gaps are and where they can elevate their thinking.

Tip 3: Sweat the Details as You Fashion Your Argument

Pulitzer Prize–winning author Elizabeth Strout wrote: "As a novelist, I like the contained drama and complexity of the courtroom."[5] These are words to live by when creating thought leadership, as well. As with a good court-room lawyer, the argument should be gripping enough to hold the audience's interest, and the facts behind it persuasive.

That argument needs to be constructed piece by piece. Start by laying out the facts of the case. Using the thesis statement that you've created, identify the core problem your research will address. Then list the complicating factors. What has made this problem hard to solve? This is one time when complication is a good thing: If the problem is easy to solve, there's little point writing about it.

From there, detail the impact this problem is having and on whom. Discuss how teams have traditionally tried to solve the problem and where these solutions have fallen short. Be as specific as you can. For every assertion, challenge yourself to show why this is so, layering in evidence to support your argument in the form of data and examples.

Now, lay out your "aha moments." These are the insights that you plan to share. Not every idea has to be new, but you should have several that are fresh and differentiating. Your "aha moment" could simply involve exploring the right questions that can help your audience diagnose an issue or benchmark their performance more effectively.

Many authors run out of gas when they hit this stage. One reason is that it's easier to be descriptive and report on a problem than it is to come up with a new response to it. But fatigue is also to blame. Many authors leave the task of crafting insights and actions for the end – and run out of steam before they get there. And if they're already tired of the topic, imagine how the reader will feel.

Here are some ways to add "oomph" to your argument:

- *Stay true to your brand:* If robust research and analysis are foundational strengths for your thought leadership organization, lean into them. If strategy or application is where your organization can show its muscle, concentrate on those areas. The thought leadership that results will be more credible – and the audience will see the difference.

- *Strengthen your core:* As we mentioned in Chapter 4, there are a few main areas in which thought leadership–producing organizations can gain differentiation: data, analysis, and strategic or technical expertise. Some organizations can be great in one or two areas, but rarely do they excel in all three, given the high competitive bar and level of commitment required to sustain it. Building on foundational strengths gives the publishing organization the opportunity to expand their core areas of excellence over time, taking on different topics and more varied analyses.

- *Be provocative:* Credibility depends less on being unquestionably right and more on being intellectually rigorous – and curious. While expressing a unique point of view can invite ridicule or criticism, thinking independently can inspire respect. Bold ideas – backed by reliable data – spark more stimulating conversation, as long as the authors have the courage of their convictions. Authors should avoid de-risking their narrative to such a point that it becomes bland and uninspiring. What business readers – and ultimately business buyers – are looking for is a true thought partner, someone willing to think creatively and test convention. So, be prepared to question the deep-seated presumptions in the industry or function or practice you're writing about. Does your data uncover any cracks in that logic? If so, what would be an interesting way to make that case?

- *Be useful:* Authors sometimes fret that offering specific guidance can give away their organization's "secret sauce." But such concerns are usually ill-founded. Pragmatism wins more hearts and minds than abstract prescriptions. Take 30,000-foot thinking down to sea level and anticipate the questions leaders and implementers would have. You're not creating an instruction manual, but helping readers see what success looks like – and how they can get there – differentiates your content. "Next day" actions can give readers the clear, actionable guidance most business leaders crave. If these actions are aligned to the producing organization's expertise, prescriptive thought leadership can provide an on-ramp for future engagement.

- *Stress-test your story:* Present your thought leadership to a smart person outside of the business environment you wrote it for and see if they understand it. In fact, see if they can get through it! Similarly, if the thought leadership is on a more technical topic, present it to someone non-technical. It's far better to challenge your own content internally first than to wait until you're presenting publicly to a room full of experts to see superficialities exposed.

- *Be ready for anything:* It's one thing to present research findings and recommendations to an executive team. But if a leader gets really engaged, they will ask probing questions that your data hasn't answered. This is a good thing. Even though you won't have all the answers, you can tap related research and analysis to address business problems. And it can point you toward the next research project you might undertake. Advancing the dialog is part of the process.

Tip 4: Start Writing, and When You Think You're Done, Start Again

First and second drafts are the hardest to write, since this is where most of the mental tussling happens. But many authors make the mistake of stopping once they have a solid draft, assuming their work is done. This deprives them of the all-important edit. "There's a lot of mechanical work to writing," Ernest Hemingway is often credited with telling a 19-year-old aspiring writer who was also his deckhand. "There is, and you can't get out of it. I rewrote the first part of *A Farewell to Arms* at least fifty times. You've got to work it over. The first draft of anything is sh**."[6] We won't repeat the last word, but you get the message.

Despite the pain of revision, a good edit allows muscle memory to take hold. For example, those who have experienced the agony of losing a document in a computer crash may have found that recreating the draft from scratch took a fraction of the original time and delivered a more fluid and readable result. That's because our brains have synthesized the core information and can now place it on the page in a more concise and articulate way.

Once you're done with your edit, it's time to edit again. But this time, someone else should hold the pen. All good thought leadership functions should engage a pool of editors who can look at content with an objective eye and polish prose, as well as identify and correct inconsistencies and circular logic. Their professional touch can work wonders, but only if authors are open to feedback – instead of enamored with their own words.

One trick editors use is to read the piece aloud. Doing so can help writers create a cadence and strike the right conversational tone. Academic sentences and comma-filled lists can trip a tongue, showing writers where they must streamline their language. Reading aloud can also reveal where ideas still need to be unpacked, where the connections made in the mind were lost in the writing process. It also reveals where sections drone on. Simplicity is a beautiful thing when it comes to thought leadership.

After the basic cleanup, editors also review for other key elements, including:

- *A catchy hook:* In journalism, reporters spend a lot of energy designing their leading statement or "lede." They know they only have a second or two to capture the reader's attention and entice them to read more. In thought leadership, the hook tries to do the same, recognizing that if senior executives don't sense value quickly, they'll move on. The original thesis statement is a good breeding ground for possible hook ideas. For instance, playing off the thesis developed about women leaders in the workplace, authors might say, "It took 10 years and millions of dollars of investment to launch a rocket to the moon, but advancing women into positions of corporate leadership is taking far longer, costs less, and requires no rocket science. Why is this problem harder to solve?

- *The people part of the story:* It's more interesting to read about an individual or team than a nameless, faceless entity. Using the personalization technique is what makes writers and speakers like Malcolm Gladwell or Adam Grant so good at what they do. Where it makes sense, personalize the exposition – give the characters in your story a name, even if the name is simply "the head of procurement" or a "forensic accountant and young financial analyst." Detail the specific problem they face or their aspiration. You don't need pages and pages to set the scene: a few well-crafted lines will generally do the trick. But the more viscerally we can place the reader in the shoes of our audience, the more everyone will care about the story and the more the conclusions will stick.

- *A change in fortune:* The brain pays attention when things go from good to bad or bad to good. If we've created a sympathetic protagonist, we'll want to know "what happens next." A couple of details on the triggering circumstance and how the individual or group dealt with the events that transpired make a story memorable. This is where case studies are useful.

- *Signposts along the way:* The best murder mysteries include some healthy foreshadowing to build suspense and give the reader a reason to stick around. A piece of thought leadership should be no different. An author could open a piece by stating, "90% of transformations fail because they don't involve front-line personnel in the change process." The piece could then go on to tell the story of what happened, describing the experiences of a particular company or team and how it drove meaningful change by tapping the power and influence of front-line employees. Signposting can also hold readers' attention, because they don't have to imagine where the author might be taking them.

Tip 5: Use Images to Tell Parts of the Story Most Persuasively

The human brain processes images far faster than words. In fact, a team of MIT neuroscientists found that it takes our brains just 13 milliseconds to infer the meaning from a photo or chart, whereas reading a 100- to 200-word text description can take the average person a full minute.[7] While visual stimuli have served as a source of essential information for sighted creatures throughout the millennia, written communication has only existed for a few thousand years. So it makes sense that our brains are more adept at processing image-based content.

Our research also overwhelmingly showed that senior business readers value visuals.

The most effective imagery extends the conversation – rather than repeating basic points made in the narrative, makes the content more memorable, and increases the chances that it will be shared. That may be why Visual Capitalist, an infographic-producing organization that "stands for a world where data can be better understood by everyone" has a monthly audience of eight million people.[8]

Chapter 9

Optimizing a Thought Leadership Operating Model

Organizations grow organically, adding roles and capabilities as new needs arise. And thought leadership organizations tend to be lean, with each individual wearing multiple hats. However, as the organization evolves, leaders may need to adjust how teams are investing their time. To make the biggest impact, your content engine must be a well-oiled machine.

Traditional thought leadership organizational structures will likely take many different forms as both enterprise producers and individual thought leaders determine the best way to integrate, incorporate, and manage generative AI. Even as executives work the technology into operating models, the most effective thought leadership will always be intentionally holistic – aligned with the parent organization's brand and business strategy – and functioning as the foundation for marketing, communications, PR, and sales campaigns. At the same time, content must remain independent and objective to deliver the maximum benefit.

Striking the right balance requires an engaged steering team that understands both internal business objectives and external client needs. Defining a "strategy squad" of senior leaders helps ensure alignment – and builds buy-in for thought leadership at the organization's highest levels.

Focusing disparate teams around shared strategic goals – and assigning leaders that can light the way – keeps messaging consistent and consolidates brand voice. It can also prevent redundancy and boost quality by enabling strategic alignment and cross-team collaboration right from the start.

If we were to build a new thought leadership organization today, knowing everything we know now, here's how the pieces would be connected – and how work would be distributed:

- **The Ideas Lab** builds the content portfolio, gaining buy-in from business leadership and ensuring alignment with corporate objectives and strategy.

- **The Research and Analytics Hub** manages data collection, surveying, and analysis, tapping both proprietary data and collaborating with partner research firms as well as integrating synthetic data as appropriate for the organization's use of generative AI. The Hub ensures research rigor and analytical authority through all iterations of the content development.

- **The Storytelling Wing** creates the content in all forms, from whitepapers to infographics to video, audio, or digital experiences. This team understands how to deliver data-driven insight in a consumable, compelling, and interesting way. They know when and how to use generative AI content development tools in an appropriate, impactful, and ethical manner.

- **The Production and Distribution Engine** delivers the final assets. It equips account teams, sellers, and teams across the organization with the right content in the right format, enabling everyone to use it with the right clients or prospects at the right time. Depending on the size and remit of this group, it might also manage external client or user engagement through press releases, newsletter, email promotions, social media, advertising, and other promotions.

- **The Legal and Governance Protectorate** ensures that the thought leadership production process, final content, and promotional activities are sound, defensible, and sustainable, whether or not they include the use of generative AI.

Figure 9.1 Thought leadership operating model.

A new way to think about building a thought leadership operation

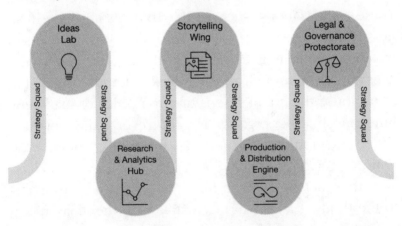

Now that we've outlined the specific roles these groups should play, let's examine each in greater detail.

Ideas Lab

The Ideas Lab is where the thought leadership content portfolio is strategized and executed. Depending on the

Optimizing a Thought Leadership Operating Model

size of the organization, this lab could be structured as an agile squad or, at the other end of the spectrum, a permanently staffed department. But even the smallest Ideas Lab would need at least one permanent or continuous staff member: a thought leadership executive that ranks high enough to own and manage a department budget, make strategy decisions, and pull teams together as needed to produce thought leadership assets.

The thought leadership executive creates and maintains the content portfolio and, depending on the size of the producing department, may create detailed project schedules and assign and oversee resources, as well. In large professional services organizations, the thought leadership function often stands alone as a "think tank" that preserves essential independence from the commercial enterprise. These organizations, such as the IBM Institute for Business Value, McKinsey Global Institute, BCG Henderson Institute, Capgemini Research Institute, and others, deliver authority through research-based thought leadership as in-house think tanks, separate from sales or marketing functions. In other organizations however, a thought leadership function might report into marketing, communications, research, or operations.

Other members of the Ideas Lab could report directly to the thought leadership executive – or they may report to other leaders with a dotted line into the Ideas Lab. At a minimum, the Ideas Lab should include the following contributing staff members:

- The head of the Research and Analytics Hub, who should bring a data-first perspective to idea generation and portfolio development. This leader ensures that research is used as the foundation of original thought leadership. They should ensure data is collected and used thoroughly to fuel the content engine, while also avoiding duplication and waste. They should also track that the right technologies, including traditional analytics and generative AI, are used to maximize investments in data collection and analysis.

- A lead from the Storytelling Wing, who assigns editorial talent, will need to review content against portfolio priorities. Like the research and analytics leader, the storytelling lead should identify new technologies – such as generative AI – and incorporate them into the storytelling process at the right time and in the right way. This leader is also responsible for reviewing and approving final content.

- The design lead from the Production and Distribution Engine serves as creative director, ensuring early visibility into whether design templates can be used to save time or custom design is needed to promote specific points of differentiation.

- The deployment lead from the Production and Distribution Engine creates plans for content promotion, aligning with the enterprise marketing teams to support individual and collective brand and demand generation goals.

- One or two liaisons from the organization's promotions arm, such as marketing, communications, PR, analyst relations, corporate citizenship, or key strategic areas, should be on the team, as well. These liaisons integrate thought leadership into the overall corporate calendar to maximize visibility and value. They also engage stakeholders who can champion thought leadership assets and investments across the enterprise.

The members of the Ideas Lab should meet weekly, at a minimum, to review the portfolio, adjust for stakeholder delays, or accommodate urgent or emerging enterprise or societal issues. This team also adjudicates any conflicts in scheduling or priority and has the final say about which thought leadership content is produced and when it is promoted.

Those in the Ideas Lab should also spend time each week scouring the competition's social media feeds and consuming thought leadership produced by other organizations. They also will likely need access to market analytics, such as popular SEO keyword searches, to learn which topics are generating the most engagement.

The Ideas Lab is responsible for deliverables that will be used by both the thought leadership organization and other groups or functions across the enterprise, including:

- The thought leadership portfolio, including a short- and long-term schedule, with detailed information about the content scheduled to launch each quarter. Documentation should also highlight the general topics and themes that will be covered over the next 12 months.

- A prioritized set of "signature" themes that tie to major strategic initiatives or business goals, and some complementary "spin-off" concepts that allow for more specific content or topical derivatives for specific business sectors, regions, or product divisions.

- Overall thought leadership policies and procedures, as well as brand and production guidelines specific to thought leadership that align with and add value to overall corporate objectives and targets.

Research and Analytics Hub

The Research and Analytics Hub acts as the guardian of analytical quality, consistency, and rigor. Guided by a research lead, it manages data gathering and analysis, including proprietary data collection and collaboration with partner research firms. The Hub ensures analytical authority and independence across all iterations of thought leadership content development.

As we outlined in previous chapters, independent research and analysis are, by far, the top factors that motivate global executives to consume thought leadership. In the United States, 63% of executives believe that original data is the most important element driving trusted thought leadership, while only 19% say that secondary data promotes believability. This means your organization's original data is more than three times as effective in establishing trust than data you cite from other sources. This is among the most significant findings from our research: Framing your thought leadership around original research delivers a competitive advantage.

The Research and Analytics Hub takes themes generated by the Ideas Lab and determines how data and analytics can best support those concepts. The hub may recommend a new survey, a "pulsing" approach, or the use of synthetic data to get relevant research quickly. For example, they may be able to add questions to upcoming surveys that could

135

inform future thought leadership that is still in the planning phase. High-level hub visibility can help your organization extend the value of data by timing it right – and finding ways to repurpose data that boosts its ROI.

Besides its leader, the Research and Analytics Hub should be staffed by several subject matter experts:

- Survey designers who have expertise in both quantitative and qualitative techniques that can be used collectively or independently to paint the fullest possible picture. These individuals will know when to formulate surveys that use more sophisticated statistical techniques and analyses, or when simpler data approaches are more appropriate.

- Data scientists with experience in multiple analytical approaches. These individuals should wake up every morning thinking about new ways to squeeze meaningful insights from survey responses and efficient ways to condense thousands of open-ended comments into concise quotable summaries. Determining whether to employ basic frequency, multivariate analysis, max diff, predictive modeling, or myriad other techniques, including a fantastically named favorite: sigmoid squishification.

- Research analysts who are so familiar with the data that they know instantly whether it is being reflected accurately as content is being developed or during data validation, which is an essential part of the quality control process.

- Market analysts who scour the press and academic journals for the latest insights on what's new and what's next. These experts find joy in meshing your organization's original proprietary research with broader market data to make observations about what's happening in the field – and predict what changes are brewing.

Members of the Research and Analytics Hub amass data from internal, external, and bespoke sources and partnerships. They manage data efficiently and intelligently, using data lakes or "libraries" to house reusable raw data and analytical assets. They create "sandboxes" where they can play and experiment with different data collection techniques and analytical models. They are also orchestrators of new technologies and conduits for how they can be deployed into thought leadership processes. For example, this team is responsible for finding the best way to incorporate large language models and generative AI into data collection, analysis, and inference approaches. These individuals should also be experts in bringing research to life with data visualizations, transforming dry data into exciting, accessible insights.

In some organizations, the Research and Analytics Hub might also be responsible for tracking KPIs and measuring the performance of the thought leadership practice, which we explore further in Chapter 11.

Storytelling Wing

The Storytelling Wing understands how to deliver data-driven insight in a consumable, compelling, and interesting way. Teams can create top-notch thought leadership in whatever form it takes: a report or whitepaper, a long-form infographic or short-form data visualization, a video, a podcast, or an immersive digital experience.

Historically, the Storytelling Wing has been staffed by writers and editors with experience crafting academic research papers, corporate marketing materials, or journalistic feature stories. Since ChatGPT burst onto the scene in November 2022 – quickly becoming the fastest growing consumer application in history[1] – this role has evolved.

Recent research on the impact of generative AI[2] shows that marketing jobs – in particular, content creation jobs – are at high risk of replacement and augmentation by AI technologies and tools. Some leaders now see writers and editors as prompt engineers, humanity injectors, fact checkers – or simply want them to justify their existence. Recent research among CMOs found that the percentage of revenue earmarked for the creation and delivery of content is expected to shrink by 20% over the next two years.[3] But these are still early days, and the impact of generative AI on content creators is still to be fully understood.

As we outlined in Chapter 4, one of the key features of thought leadership is uniqueness. And, by its nature, generative AI can only reflect the knowledge it was trained on – meaning content that already exists. Therefore, a bot can't produce a unique perspective – at least for now. In his *Almost Timely News* newsletter, Christopher Penn described it this way, "More often than not, they [large language models and generative AI] create mediocre to good results, but rarely excellent and never unique, never-before-seen results. That's because their nature is an averaging of what already exists, tuned to deliver above average results."[4]

Despite the uncertain long-term future of human content creators, the current consensus is that today's thought leadership still requires a human touch. Still, your organization's storytellers should become intimately familiar with generative AI tools and how they can help improve content development. They need to understand the benefits and limitations of generative AI tools because, while generative AI might not replace your content development staff, people who know how to use generative AI to produce better results will replace those who don't.

The Storytelling Wing should include:

- Writers who can listen to a presentation, conduct an interview, or attend a meeting and turn what they hear into a cohesive, comprehensive, and consumable asset. These individuals look forward to starting with a blank page and crafting a new narrative. They can interrogate the data, accentuate the analysis, shape a distinctive angle, and develop a strong argument – all things that generative AI cannot yet do. These people aren't easy to find, but they are worth their weight in gold for a thought leadership–producing organization.

- Editors who might hate to start from scratch but are experts at taking what's already on the page and turning it into a story others would pay to read, even if they don't have to.

- Proofreaders who have an opinion on the Oxford comma, know the difference between its and it's, and aren't afraid to share funny grammatical memes on LinkedIn. These people can't help but find mistakes in everything they read – including this book, most likely.

- Partners from other parts of the organization, usually marketing or communications, who can join storyline brainstorming meetings, provide access to client or customer insights and case studies, and engage with interview prospects. They can also serve as emissaries to the rest of the organization, sharing early research results that can be incorporated into campaigns, press releases, event presentations, and client pitches.

The Storytelling Wing takes outputs from the research and analytics hub and crafts the thought leadership thesis. They shape the initial outline, gather input from stakeholders, and oversee the story creation process from first draft to final product. They ensure alignment with corporate storylines and incorporate quotes and case studies while maintaining the independence that comes from building thought leadership on a foundation of outside-in, data-driven research.

Storytellers are responsible for delivering thought leadership in multiple forms. Some organizations have a practice large enough to have specialists drafting long-form reports, short-form data stories or infographics, presentation or video scripts, blog posts, articles, or social media posts. Some organizations use generative AI tools such as Jasper.ai (https://www.jasper.ai), CloserCopy (https://www.closerscopy.com), Writesonic (https://writesonic.com), Copysmith (https://copysmith.ai), Grammarly (https://www.grammarly.com), or Writer (https://writer.com) to augment human storytellers for some of the content types. And some organizations have one busy human who has to do it all.

To strengthen their bench of editorial talent, many organizations invest in a pool of writers and then establish a writing mentorship program to gain scale. These programs can develop talent, with senior staff coaching junior teammates. They can also raise awareness of what authentic thought leadership should look like to improve the quality of content across the board. Organizations should also invest in generative AI training for content creators to boost productivity. Learning and experimentation may take time away from content development, but it's essential to build a modern thought leadership practice.

Thought Leadership, Generative AI, and Data Governance

Storytelling used to be a low-tech operation. But pen and paper – or keyboard and monitor – no longer suffice. Today's storytellers need access to generative AI tools, but they must be provided with the appropriate guardrails.

This is one of the top barriers organizations face in adopting new generative AI applications. In June 2023, our research found that 61% of CEOs are concerned about data lineage or provenance when it comes to generative AI. Forty percent see traceability and recognition of intellectual property as a particular concern. To overcome these challenges, generative AI implementation teams will need to navigate multiple data privacy and IP rules as they train and tune generative AI applications, which have been built based on various foundation models.

Some organizations have faced potential lawsuits focused on the data they used to train their large language models. From newspapers to novelists, content creators argue that they should have a say in how their content is used – and that they should be paid fairly for this exchange.[5]

Before you encourage your storytellers to harness the power of generative AI, make sure you have the necessary governance processes in place. Writers and editors should be able to answer each of these questions about the content they've created using generative AI:

- Have you used generative AI to inspire, summarize, or improve your content, instead of using what it created wholesale?

- Has another person on the team checked your gen AI-produced work for bias?

- Have you validated any facts provided by generative AI using other primary sources?

- Have you searched online to see if the content you've created using generative AI stands out from what has already been published?

If the storytelling team answers "no" to any of these questions, your organization should create stronger guidelines regarding the use of generative AI – and make sure everyone on the team understands what is expected of them.

Production and Distribution Engine

This Production and Distribution Engine wraps content in ribbons and bows, packaging the organization's expertise in a way that drives engagement and encourages loyalty to the thought leadership brand. Whether the goal is building a pipeline of prospects or securing client commitment, the Production and Distribution Engine turns content created by the Storytelling Wing into a thought leadership experience. Depending on the size and scope of the group, they might aim to equip account-facing teams with "door openers" to enable client conversations or they might manage external engagement through press releases, social media, advertising, and other promotions.

This team could consist of several specialists who focus on a single aspect of production or distribution. Or it could include a few generalists who wear multiple hats. Either way, the Production and Distribution Engine needs the following capabilities:

- Design: In the age of generative AI, curiosity and a willingness to experiment will set leading design teams apart. While thought leadership has traditionally been a "white paper" or research report, today's content types are much broader. They can range from meaty reports supported by a few charts and graphs to visual journeys that sprinkle text lightly throughout. In most cases, there will be the need for a design team that can wield Adobe Illustrator and InDesign, but also other video, audio, presentation, webinar/podcast, social, and generative AI tools, such as Stable Diffusion (https://stability.ai), Midjourney (https://www.midjourney.com/home), Adobe Firefly (https://www.adobe.com/products/firefly.html), DALL·E (https://openai.com/dall-e-3). This team is most often led by a creative director, who also serves as a liaison from the production and distribution engine to the Ideas Lab.

- Production: This team directs traffic. Staffed by project managers, scrum masters, producers, and other schedule experts, they keep publication and promotion on schedule. The production team also coordinates with any partner organizations used for printing, campaign development, media placement, or event planning. In smaller organizations, this function may be assigned to someone in the Ideas Lab, the Research and Analysis Hub, or the Storytelling Wing. Whomever leads, the production function needs to ensure that assets are produced to the right specifications for posting on the web or social media, or for presentation printing, or other use. The production lead must be linked to the larger enterprise production operation as well, to ensure that thought leadership assets are available to teams that want to use them in campaign development or other promotions.

- Promotion: Ideally, the promotions function can be integrated into the thought leadership operation as part of the Production and Distribution Engine. In smaller organizations, this function might be part of the larger enterprise marketing, communications, media or analyst relations groups, the web team, or all of the above. Whether stand-alone or shared, promotions are critical to the thought leadership operation. More detail on promotions can be found in Chapter 10, but essentially, this is the megaphone you can use to get your content in front of your target audience.

Deliverables from the Production and Distribution Engine include all thought leadership content assets, from traditional research reports to videos and event presentations to podcasts, media releases, and infographics. The types of thought leadership your organization produces are only limited by the imagination, capability, and budget of your team.

Legal and Governance Protectorate

In the abstract, governance relates to how things get done: the processes and activities around how thought leadership is conceived, developed, advanced, completed, and deployed. In this way, the Legal and Governance Protectorate ensures that thought leadership development processes, published content, and promotions are sound, defensible, and sustainable. This group checks that thought leadership complies with the organization's standards, satisfies intellectual property and other regulatory requirements, and aligns with messages approved for external distribution.

For example, regarding data, governance might focus on how data is collected, stored, and protected; how survey respondents are sourced and compensated; and how survey results are shared with the rest of the organization or ecosystem partners.

In addition, governance practices need to address the independence of thought leadership content, keeping it separate from but aligned to the enterprise's commercial pursuits. Helping teams walk the line can go a long way to boosting the ROI of thought leadership (see Chapter 4 on independence for more insight into this important aspect of any thought leadership).

This team should also weigh in on content review and development processes. These might include:

- Who in the organization can direct – or dictate – what thought leadership topics are selected?

- Who is required – or allowed – to participate in content reviews?

- Who has the authority to replace a piece of thought leadership if it conflicts with parent organization messaging (even if it is based on original data)?

- Who can initiate a thought leadership project even if it isn't a priority (read: pet project) or doesn't appear on an approved through leadership calendar?

Members of the Legal and Governance Protectorate are likely "borrowed labor" from the parent organization or are contracted through organizations that hire fractional executives. At a minimum, you will need legal counsel – an attorney that specializes in intellectual property, trademark, and brand protection who can craft standard documents, such as author, speaker, or quote approval forms and collaboration or co-branding agreements. The attorney may also weigh in on language use when highly sensitive or controversial topics are covered. More consistently, they'll answer operational FAQs that highlight data and trademark protection policies, generative AI governance, email or social media engagement guidelines, and reprint rights, among others.

Strategy Squad

The Strategy Squad is the team of senior business leaders that steers thought leadership enterprise wide. This group should include customer-facing and business unit leaders who can help advise on burning issues and surface high-value topics that align with the strategy and goals of the parent business. This should be an ad hoc group from across the organization that meets regularly, but not frequently – perhaps only once or twice a year.

This team should define the organization's strategic direction – and take a portfolio approach to thought leadership content development.

The Strategy Squad should also inform the content approach, highlighting where content targeted to specific industries, job roles, or functional areas might give thought leadership research longer legs. Most research studies include a great deal of data – more than any single piece of content should showcase, and more than you could or should ask your readers to consume in a single report. A content derivative strategy can keep valuable insights from ending up on the cutting room floor – and help the organization get more value from its research investments.

Another important consideration for the Strategy Squad is how much content will be available for users without commitment. This team will need to take a position on whether users will need to provide their contact information in exchange for your thought leadership content, commonly known as content gating.

To gate or not to gate, that is the question. And how your organization answers this question, explicitly or implicitly, reveals the role it expects thought leadership content to play – a short-term lead generator or a longer-term brand and demand builder.

One key consideration is that gating content positions thought leadership closer to marketing, which makes it appear less independent. This approach can limit the added value thought leadership delivers to your business (see Chapter 4 on the independence premium). On the other hand, not gating may be seen by your organization as a missed opportunity to gather information about thought leadership users who find your information valuable.

Gating content has come in and out of fashion over the years. Today, most prominent thought leadership organizations do not gate digital content across the board. One reason is that gating increases abandonment. That is, readers find and click on the site but leave without engaging because they decline to provide contact information to get it. This fact hasn't stopped marketers in pursuit of the almighty lead, but it may be part of the reason that marketing ROI is 16 times lower than the returns delivered by thought leadership.

Most thought leadership professionals have strong views against gating. However, there is a middle ground, and some will agree to gating downloadable (usually PDF) assets. Staunch non-gaters can sometimes be swayed if (and only if) ALL of the thought leadership content is available – ungated – in digital form, generally on your website. When this is the case, that means the main course, the meat of your thought leadership, is available without commitment, but if a reader wants it in a takeaway bag, they need to provide their email address in exchange. In thought leadership, gating should be used sparingly, carefully, and only for a very specific purpose with quantified performance goals that can be tracked and evaluated – and the gates can be eliminated if metrics show they are preventing your audience from finding and engaging with your content.

Another important consideration for your Strategy Squad is how to mention and link to your own company in your thought leadership. Some organizations feature their own expertise, quoting internal experts in their reports (see KPMG's *The Decarbonization Journey: Five Pillars to Achieving Net Zero*[6]). Some organizations feature their own experiences as a case study in their thought leadership (see IBM Institute for Business Value's *The Revolutionary Content Supply Chain*)[7] while others avoid it. In their regular *White Space* report, Source Global[8] typically advocates for explicit on-ramps to offerings.

Once your thought leadership operating model is in place, each team can be scaled up or down depending on the size of an organization. It's not the number of people or systems that matter as much as the skillsets, capabilities, and handoffs that move content from one stage to the next. Getting the mechanics right – and keeping teams in lockstep – is what will allow your team to deliver thought leadership that will drive better business performance.

Thought Leadership Operating Model and Workflow for Smaller Organizations

When it comes to building and sustaining a thought leadership capability, the operational elements and general workflows are the same for large and small enterprises alike. It's just a matter of scale.

No organization, regardless of size, can skip any element of the thought leadership operating model. While larger organizations may develop in-house capability for some elements – including ideation, research and analysis, storytelling, production, and distribution, legal and governance, and strategy – smaller organizations may find it most effective to tap their partner ecosystem to fill some of these roles.

Perhaps you have excellent relationships with some key clients and you're confident they would be willing to share their experiences and outcomes with you. If that's the case, incorporate their expertise into your thought leadership through case studies or interviews, so this type of thought leadership might be differentiating and compelling for your target audience – in addition to being cost-effective and manageable for your organization. Other organizations might struggle to build these types of relationships with clients and will need to find endorsements another way.

If you've collaborated with a client on thought leadership, its marketing team may also be willing to promote the study as part of the company's campaigns. You may also be able to find affordable freelance social media professionals. Or, if there's a university nearby, marketing professors may be able to connect you with promising students that need practical, real-world experience.

Partnering with a related professional association or not-for-profit organization in the development and promotion of thought leadership can have dual benefits. First, non-profits are often seen as less biased than commercial enterprises,[9] so partnering with them can give your thought leadership an air of independence, which delivers a higher ROI (see Chapter 4). Second, these organizations are often staff-rich and resource-poor, which means companies are in a good position to tap their expertise, if they bring something of value to the table.

Another option is to build the capabilities you need from the ground up. However, if you're part of a smaller organization and decide to cultivate internal talent, it's important to guard against thought leadership devolving into hobbyism. It's very easy for people to gravitate toward topics that interest them, forgetting that the best thought leadership content is aligned with and supports strategic business objectives. Governance remains essential, no matter the size or structure of the thought leadership producing operation.

With respect to data and research, smaller organizations may want to start with simple, manageable studies. Large surveys can cost hundreds of thousands of dollars. And the more demographic parameters you want to address, the higher the cost – sometimes into the millions of dollars. A smaller, self-service survey on a topic relevant to the organization's business could be the best bet for a smaller enterprise.

But it's important to remember that a thought leadership program is nothing if it's not built on a foundation of credibility and trust. That's why you must always err on the side of integrity in everything you do in thought leadership. That means protecting the privacy of individuals and organizations that participate in your primary research, ensuring the accuracy of your data analysis, and providing unique conclusions and recommendations. And don't forget to disclose when and how generative AI tools are used throughout the thought leadership production process.

The lessons of thought leadership from larger organizations also apply to smaller ones. For example, you need to be consistent in your financial and resource commitment. Resist the temptation to reduce or cut off support if your thought leadership investments don't deliver immediate returns. A thorough leadership approach is a long-term relationship development and brand building effort – and this book is the first time we're aware of that the value of thought leadership has been quantified.

That means there's zero chance of succeeding with a thought leadership program that's measured like a short-term marketing campaign. But if you set long-term goals, commit to your strategy, invest appropriately, and build relationships with internal and external partners, there are many riches to be won – for small and large organizations alike.

Tips for Individual Thought Leaders

Becoming a thought leader can help professionals advance their careers – and increase their personal eminence. By staying current on business and market trends and sharing the insights they uncover, individual thought leaders can be a source of trusted intelligence that people feel inspired to follow.

But building a rock-solid reputation requires more than just social media reshares. To be successful, you must identify and capitalize on those things that make you unique. Ask yourself: Why would a busy professional be willing to spend their valuable time engaging with my content or ideas?

The three primary levers of thought leadership that we outlined earlier can help you answer this question. Here's how individuals can pull these levers to develop a personal brand that attracts and influences an ever-growing audience.

Uniqueness

Sharpen your point of view so that each piece you create stands out in a flooded market. Define what makes your perspective unique, whether that's your background, experience, or approach, then offer advice that only you could provide. Develop your personal voice so that your content is easily recognized. Don't be afraid to showcase your style! People choose to engage with creators based on their personalities and opinions, so be sure to let yours shine through. Use generative AI to speed up the content creation process but don't give in to the temptation to cut and paste. Edit heavily to avoid rehashing old ideas or publishing something that comes off as canned. It might work for a short while, but your audience will quickly see through this thin veil and lose trust in your content. As we've seen time and again, professional reputations take a lifetime to build – and only a moment to destroy.[10]

Quality

Push yourself to go beyond publishing opinion pieces, even if they offer actionable advice. Audiences want to see hard data that supports your viewpoint – and they want that data to be as fresh as possible. While it is possible for individuals to conduct independent research, it will likely be more cost-effective to cite secondary sources. Select those sources carefully, however, digging into research methodology to ensure the data you're amplifying is valid and defensible. Interviewing relevant experts can also help you capture objective, newsworthy insights. However you choose to build your argument, keep it independent and free of commercial messaging. The quality of your content will suffer if it sounds like a sales pitch.

Reach

Publishing thought leadership won't help your career if it's trapped inside an echo chamber. Build your network by clearly defining your target audience and connecting with people who fit the profile. Engage with these professionals online by liking, commenting on, and resharing relevant posts on social platforms. In-person conferences and networking events also offer a great opportunity to make meaningful connections. Build trust with your growing audience through consistency, reliability, and careful content curation. Whether you reach out to them on a regular cadence or only when you have something new to say, make sure that your communications encourage them to continue the conversation, both with you and within their own networks. The more compelled they are to share your thought leadership with others, the larger your audience will grow.

Chapter 10

Engaging With Targeted Business Leaders

It's a great time to be a thought leader. In the past 18 months, executives have increased their consumption of thought leadership by a whopping 50%. They now spend just a few minutes shy of three hours each week with the business content that makes them smarter. That's more time than many leaders spend with each of their direct reports.[1]

This shift gives thought leadership–producing organizations an even larger window for capturing their share of the $100 billion opportunity.

However, the time business leaders spend consuming thought leadership tends to be focused: they typically access content from five thought leadership content producers. They also stick with the organizations they trust most, which tend to be those that are more independent and less commercial.

But producing brilliant thought leadership is only half the battle. The other half is getting it in front of the right audience at the right time and in the right format. Without a promotions program that's as amazing as the content it amplifies, thought leadership investments fall flat.

Three Engagement Approaches

So how do you get your thought leadership in front of your audience? There are dozens of distribution channels to choose from, and the most effective mix will be different for each organization.

However, it's helpful to start by considering the different types of communications needed to pull people deeper into the engagement funnel. As you craft your strategy, you will probably want to include tactics and channels that incorporate three distinct engagement approaches.

1. **One-to-many:** A thought leadership producer takes a mass communications approach. This involves distributing high-level messaging to a large, general audience.

2. **One-to-few:** A producer adopts a segmentation strategy that targets specific groups, such as CEOs, technology specialists, or users in a particular geography or industry. People who have previously consumed thought leadership on a particular topic could be a segment as well. Content is targeted to the group's collective profile.

3. **One-to-one:** Truly personalized content is tailored to an individual in formats and channels that are specific to their unique preferences.

Figure 10.1 Three distinct thought leadership engagement approaches.

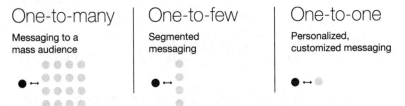

One-to-many	One-to-few	One-to-one
Messaging to a mass audience	Segmented messaging	Personalized, customized messaging

One-to-Many: Mass Communication

One-to-many engagement reaches large – and largely unknown – audiences, some of whom might be potential clients or customers. Most traditional forms of engagement fall into this category, as do social media, podcasts, and webinars. Here are specific strategies to help amplify thought leadership across seven key mass communication channels.

Press Releases

Many smaller thought leadership-producing organizations bypass press releases because they fear their efforts will be overshadowed by big PR firms. That's a mistake. As news organizations continue to cut their reporting staff and struggle to retain advertising revenue, many of them are desperate for content to fill their publications. Thought leadership helps them fill extra column inches, whether that's in a print or digital publication.

Any time your thought leadership has a news angle, you should send a press release, even if it's only to a few journalists that specifically cover your field or industry. If your thought leadership is based on new, proprietary data, or it offers a unique perspective on persistent problems or current events, it can make a harried journalist's life easier.

If you help an editor fill space with interesting, trusted content, you've made a friend. And the more media relationships you can build, the better. If budget allows, consider using "wires," or distribution services such as Reuters, to get your content in front of as many journalists as possible.

Press release aggregators come in two major forms: free aggregators that let you add your organization's content and hope for the best, or paid aggregators that let you target your content to a more specific audience. Free press release aggregators, including PRLog (https://www.prlog.org), openPR (https://www.openpr.com), or IssueWire (https://www.issuewire.com), provide a variety of digital engagement services, such as forwarding content to various search engines, tracking daily activity, auditing SEO, and spam protection. Paid press release aggregators[2] offer similar services but also provide access to pre-defined media types, such as major urban dailies, business press, or industry- or country-specific outlets that your clients and prospects are more likely to consume.

Bylined Articles

In addition to sending press releases that inspire independent reporting, many successful thought leadership organizations encourage their authors to write "bylined" articles that are published with their names attached. This type of content, which often summarizes thought leadership research and connects it to a current or upcoming market moment, is also known as "earned placement."

Many publications accept unsolicited manuscripts, including traditional news magazines and newspapers (such as *Fortune* or the *Financial Times*), business publications (such as *Harvard Business Review*), academic journals (such as *Journal of International Management* or *Gender and Society*), professional association magazines (such as *PM Network* for the project management profession or *IEEE Spectrum* for engineers), as well as online publications (such as Buzzfeed or Medium).

Some publications will have much more rigorous standards and requirements for content than others. Some placements may be easier to secure if your authors partner with known writers or editors who work regularly with the publication. And some are strictly pay for play – such as the Fast Company Executive Board.

The challenges in this area include difficulty in establishing and maintaining relationships with journalists or editors. Plus, bylines are typically edited by the publication, requiring authors to be flexible when it comes to word choice and style. Especially in print publications, lead times can also be extraordinarily long. You may have to be patient, but bylines can boost your credibility when the opportunity pans out.

Advertising Campaigns and Paid Media

Where earned placements leave off, paid placements pick up the slack. Sponsored content, for instance, gives you the chance to publish your perspective in a well-respected business publication – for a price.

This tactic can be expensive, but also effective when used as part of an overall engagement campaign that includes a constant drumbeat of content. One-off ads rarely help build the trusted relationships thought leadership

159

relies on, but a series of placements in publications popular with your target audience could help your brand establish eminence.

One common approach, which combines paid advertising and organic content marketing, is to become a regular columnist for a printed or online newspaper or magazine. Most large business publications look to columnists to augment their content portfolio in areas where they don't have in-house expertise, especially if they think the topic will be interesting to their readers.

Publishing a column often comes with a fee, but some smaller outlets may be willing to accept regular contributions without payment if it helps them feed the beast. This type of partnership lets you highlight your latest thought leadership and keeps your name relevant with and familiar to readers. A side benefit is that other media outlets will see your thought leadership, which means you might be quoted in other articles that extend your reach even further.

Social Media

Social media is now central to thought leadership engagement – but success depends on your ability to cut through the noise.

The first step is deciding which social media platforms to engage on. Without an army of people or bots, it's too time-consuming to manage more than a few platforms at a time. Most thought leadership organizations have LinkedIn accounts, groups, and pages, because it's the largest and most well-read business platform globally (though its presence is restricted in some countries). LinkedIn allows for longer posts in multiple formats, links to your original content, and has additional promotion opportunities, such as LinkedIn Live events and InMail promotions – for an additional fee. Where LinkedIn is unavailable – China, for example – WeChat (Weixin) is the most used platform.

Some organizations also use X (formerly known as Twitter), Instagram, Facebook, Pinterest, or TikTok for more frequent, shorter or more visual posts. But interaction on these platforms is often superficial, non-business-oriented, and at times nefarious. This means they aren't great for building a loyal, long-term audience.

Once you decide on a platform, do some homework before you start posting. Assess how others are using their accounts, including how often they post, how they use images, how they tag other users, and how they leverage hashtags to connect their posts with topics of interest. Check to see who usually posts from popular accounts and if multiple people tend to chime in. As you discover different approaches, you can choose the one that seems right for you. Then jump in.

Experiment with different types of posts to see what generates the kind of engagement you're looking for. Be clear about whether you're trying to build a strong follower base or just gain maximum visibility. Follow other influential organizations and re-share their posts with your own commentary.

Recent analysis suggests that brands deploying successful social media marketing strategies will likely see a 6 to 8% increase in followers each month. But these new followers may not be part of your target audience. That's why you should also consider the quality, not just quantity, of your social media engagement.

Leading social media marketing experts suggest that a good social engagement rate – which calculates the percentage of followers who like, share, or comment on your posts – should be somewhere between 1% and 5%.[3] However, it's not quite that simple, because the more followers you have, the harder it is to sustain high engagement rates. On average, you want your social content to reach somewhere between 2% and 15% of your followers, depending on the type of content posted. For instance, images and video tends to drive greater reach, so you may set higher targets for that type of content.

Email Distribution Programs

Mass email distribution programs can be used to build awareness of your thought leadership program and keep your audience up to date on your organization's latest research. Whether you're purchasing massive email lists to attract potential users or carefully curating a list of qualified subscribers, email programs give your content a chance to shine – without constraints. They let you control the timing, length, and tone and of your messaging, as well as the specific audience receiving it.

However, most people who receive your emails simply won't open them. The percentage of people who click on a subscription email, also known as the open rate, tends to be low. Click-through rates – the percentage of people who both open the email and click on a link it contains – are even lower. According to common benchmarks, and depending on your industry, average open rates range from around 20 to 35% and average click-through (or click-to-open) rates are about 2 to 3%.[4, 5]

You can grow your email subscription list by giving existing subscribers an easy way to forward the newsletter to a friend or colleague. You should also give anyone clicking a social link the opportunity to subscribe and make sure subscription buttons are placed prominently on your organization's website. With curated lists (those that are built within an existing audience), we have seen open rates higher than 50% and click-through rates approaching 10 to 15%. With purchased lists – comprised of people who aren't affiliated with the brand – rates will be lower.

Mass emails can also overwhelm your target audience. When people are inundated with emails they tend to disengage or worse: unsubscribe. When this happens, you've lost your opportunity to become a trusted source of thought leadership – so tread lightly.

Producers of thought leadership must also consider regulations when sending mass emails, as unsolicited communications can violate certain countries' rules around the use of personally identifiable information (PII). Your organization's Legal and Governance Protectorate should be engaged in any discussions about setting up an email subscription program.

Podcasts

While only 20% of executives say they consume thought leadership content through podcasts, for organizations that have FOMO (fear of missing out), podcasts can provide a compelling alternative to written content or navigating through other types of media, especially in the age of multitasking. Podcasts can be consumed while driving a car or riding a bicycle – stationary or otherwise. And since the pandemic, their popularity has exploded. There are now more than three million podcasts globally, and more than 460 million people around the world listen to these serialized audio journals.[6]

Despite the draw of this format, building an interested and relevant podcast audience is extremely challenging for thought leadership producers. This is an arena where having a unique angle and a differentiated perspective is essential.

Today's generative AI environment offers exciting new options to anchor thought leadership on a big idea in a unique format, as demonstrated by Boston Consulting Group (BCG) with its "Imagine This..." podcast,[7] which pairs a human and a conversational AI bot called GENE to interview experts and investigate potential futures and the actions CEOs might take today. This format offers a timely look at business issues through the lens of the latest disruptive technology as if it's already mainstream.

Successful long-term podcasting also requires specialized equipment and technical capabilities. If your organization is serious about initiating or expanding a thought leadership podcast thought leadership presence, you must recognize the high standards inherent in successful podcasting. People expect studio-quality recordings distributed on a regular cadence with high-profile hosts and guests – which requires real investments of money, time, and professional resources.

Webinars

The pandemic elevated the role of video conferencing in business – and made webinars central to contemporary thought leadership engagement. Recent data suggests that

95% of marketers believe webinars are vital to their marketing programs. Their popularity may be waning slightly. In late 2023, 87% of marketing leaders said they hosted at least 150 webinars each year.[8] In mid-2024, that number had dropped to 57% of marketing leaders saying they host up to 50 webinars a year.[9]

Even with the drop, marketers say they are still hosting nearly one webinar a week. Why? For starters, webinars educate audiences, build trust, and generate leads – all at a fraction of the cost of attending in-person events.

The key to hosting successful webinars is knowing your audience and choosing clear and compelling topics that will engage them – and including interactive elements, such as real-time polling or a Q&A session. Providing access to speakers or insights people can't access elsewhere is especially valuable. As with social engagement, more is not always unambiguously better. Like mass emails, webinars with more targeted audiences have better conversion rates. Those with 100 to 200 registrations tend to achieve attendance rates above 50%. But attendance rates typically fall to less than 20% for webinars with more than 200 registrations.[10]

One-to-Few: Segmented Communication

One-to-few engagement connects with targeted or segmented audience groups that are likely to contain potential clients or customers. This includes email newsletters, printed outreach or leave-behind assets, roundtable events, and thought leadership ambassador programs. Here are ways to engage specific audiences across four segmented communications channels.

Newsletters

Although newsletters are an extension of your mass distribution email program, they let you target content to specific audience segments based on their preferences. If you have the audience data needed to do this effectively, you can use newsletters to make more meaningful connections.

For instance, targeted newsletters offer a great opportunity to showcase derivative content. In our experience, as many as two-thirds of field personnel believe that data specific to a client's industry is most valuable to promote additional engagement. Embedding data visualizations and infographics into these emails can help people get immersed in your data – inspiring them to click through to read more. Case studies featuring relevant big-name brands can also encourage more click throughs, especially if the featured organization is sharing secrets to success – and can back up its story with real-world data.

Newsletters can be delivered by email or postal mail, though most organizations still using direct mail for newsletter distribution have small, regional mailing lists. When you email newsletters, most marketing platforms provide analytics that allow you to track their performance, including open rates, click-through rates, and conversions, to help you improve results over time. Constant Contact (www.constantcontact.com) offers an easy-to-use template to create email newsletters, and many organizations offer training on email newsletter production.

If you're not committed to producing newsletters on a regular cadence from day one, you may want to consider an on-demand approach. It takes a lot of time and energy to produce a high-quality newsletter on a regular schedule. It's better to publish when you have something compelling to say than to bore your audience, as the real value of a newsletter program comes from long-term relationship building.

Print Magazines, Reports, and Books

Printed thought leadership is no longer *en vogue*, as printed media is antithetical to the principles of digital-first engagement and sustainable business practices, which makes it a poor primary distribution approach. Yet despite its drawbacks, there are instances when printing thought leadership might be the best approach. A LinkedIn article titled *The Revenge of Print* explains why: "Print draws in our focus, it frames our attention, limits the extraneous and offers tangible feedback in a way a screen simply can't."[11]

The IBM Institute for Business Value uses print to anchor its high-value account relationship program, with hardcover, coffee table–style books such as *The Quantum Decade* and *The CEO's Guide to Generative AI*. The Project Management Institute's Brightline Initiative has a long history of printing books[12] with its partner Thinkers 50, which extends the life of its thought leadership.

Printed leave-behinds can help solidify in-person connections made at events or during face-to-face client engagements. Direct mail can also help you cut through the digital clutter – if your content can be easily distinguished from junk mail.

One-page or executive summaries of thought leadership can catch a client's eye with interesting top-line results. They "tease" more in-depth content to pull readers in – and make it easier for them to share what they've learned with others in their organization. And a QR code printed on the summary page is an easy way to drive interested readers to the full report or paper.

Because it is costly and requires lengthy lead times, printed thought leadership should be used only in select situations and should highlight groundbreaking research or a never-before-seen point of view. If you're going to print content, it should be able to maintain its currency for at least a year or more. Work with your printer to choose sustainably sourced and produced inks and paper products – and highlight your use of these materials in the publisher's notes.

Roundtable or Small Group Events

Whether in-person or virtual, hosting exclusive roundtable events can be truly differentiating. When you bring like-minded executives together – by invitation only – it creates an environment where they can open up and discuss their experiences, concerns, and opportunities. The insights shared can be valuable for the participants and your thought leadership-producing organization alike.

In addition to strengthening relationships with the individual executives that attend, roundtable discussions can provide the fodder for fascinating thought leadership. Quotes from these conversations – when collected with permission and approved by the source before producing the piece – can add credibility and authenticity to your content.

But remember: brilliance must be inspired. To capture quote-worthy insights, you need to keep your panelists interested. For example, including an eminent interviewer or co-panelist – such as a popular expert or personality – can liven up the conversation. Offering a pre-launch briefing of new thought leadership can also get participants thinking about the trends influencing their industry and spark new ideas about how companies can evolve.

The most successful roundtable groups often have a champion – an SME who takes personal ownership of the group. It helps if that person is charismatic and personable, but the most important factor is their willingness to commit to the group and share their expertise in the topic area. It also helps to have a program manager – someone who can attend to the details of scheduling the event: sending invitations, tracking attendance, handling the technical aspects of the event, and ensuring follow-up after each session.

If you plan to create thought leadership based on what was shared at the event, you'll need to record the session to share with content developers. Be sure to get sign-off on how insights and quotes are used from each participant – and point them to published assets so they can help with promotion and raise their own eminence.

Thought Leadership Ambassador Program

Building a cohort of thought leadership ambassadors through direct engagement, such as training and badging, can be a valuable means of expanding thought leadership impact. Most large organizations have HR groups that run professional development programs. And they're invariably looking for good training content – especially if it comes pre-packaged and aligned with their objectives.

Partnering with HR formalizes and professionalizes the use of thought leadership as an essential foundation of the client relationship-building program throughout the parent company. Establish a certification or badging program that rewards learners with badges they can post on their LinkedIn profiles or in their in-house directories to activate a lucrative ripple effect. As advocates share their achievements within their own networks, others will be inspired to consume thought leadership across the business.

If your organization doesn't have an internal learning and knowledge organization or professional development function, take a look at Credly (https://info.credly.com), which is one of the largest badging organizations. The website has a great deal of information that can help you think through this approach.

One-to-One: Personalized Communication

Truly personalized content used to be a pipe dream. The amount of data and analysis needed was simply prohibitive. But now, with generative AI, hyper-personalization is not only possible – it's becoming essential.

In 2023, 42% of CMOs[13] say scaling hyper-personalization is a marketing priority – and 64% expect to use generative AI for content personalization by 2025. What will that look like? Future possibilities are still unfolding, but we will explore three personalized distribution opportunities that you can capitalize on today: Bespoke content generation, account or sales team outreach, and direct bilateral client meetings.

Bespoke Content Generation

Creating custom content for high-profile clients may sound like a heavy lift – but generative AI can lighten the load. With the right data, models, and infrastructure in place, thought leadership teams can tap the power of this transformative technology to deliver content with a personal touch.

Each piece of thought leadership already addresses a variety of specific business challenges – and derivative content may even break down trends and solutions by industry, geography, or job role. If your organization invests in the technology needed to categorize and sort datapoints – and the associated content – by factors that are relevant to your clients, the Storytelling Wing can slice and dice your insights on-demand.

When guided by a human who understands specific client pain points, generative AI can repurpose your proprietary data and analysis for an audience of one – increasing its relevance and impressing potential clients one at a time. If executives know they can come to you for answers to the specific business questions they face every day, why would they go anywhere else?

Account or Sales Team Outreach

Account-facing or sales leaders are the people who are most likely to put content in front of clients – so thought leadership teams should build close relationships with these invaluable partners.

Personal messages to account leaders, especially from someone they know in the company's thought leadership organization, can have exponential impact. Anyone who has worked in the parent organization for any length of time will likely have contacts – maybe even intricate networks – that stretch across the business.

Just as you cultivate a list of client contacts, it's important to formalize which internal contacts you should reach out to individually when relevant thought leadership is published. The more extensive your one-to-one engagement, the bigger the ripple effect you'll create.

Direct Client Meetings

Few thought leadership teams engage directly with the clients who ultimately consume the content. That said, there are several instances where direct engagement is possible, without running up against resistance from the account teams who may be protective of client relationships.

For example, account leaders can help you recruit clients for interviews to inform future thought leadership content. They can make the introduction – and may request to be present for the interview. This process should be formalized in your Legal and Governance Protectorate, so that everyone is clear about how it should be handled. The approach should include formal outreach, scheduling and interviewing, approval, and follow-up. Be sure to send a personal thank you and follow-up with the published content so that you can continue building the relationship.

You can also engage specific clients as part of an editorial council that works with the strategy squad to prioritize topics or review content. This approach helps thought leadership organizations focus on the right topics at the right time and validates new research in meaningful ways before its general release. It also has the benefit of creating a pool of executives with experience you can tap into for future research. After you recruit clients to give you their honest feedback, engage them regularly, both within and outside scheduled meetings.

Regardless of what insights you might gather, make it your mission to develop a one-to-one relationship with each source so that you can reach out directly when you have new thought leadership to share. A personal email or note always has a better chance of being opened than any email your organization could send.

There's Nothing Magical About It

Engagement is the fabric that connects thought leadership content with the clients that create value for your organization. It's what gets your insights in front of those who can benefit from it – clients and prospects, media outlets, and your account team colleagues. There's no magic wand you can wave to make people engage with your content; it takes a portfolio mentality and long-term engagement approach. It's hard. Be ready to use every tool at your disposal to increase your impact – then watch the benefits start rolling in.

Part IV

Accountability and Outcomes

Chapter 11

Measuring Your Success

There's no single factor that defines a thought leadership program's success. Just as quality, uniqueness, and reach must each be considered when crafting thought leadership, how well you have hit those marks must be measured.

In addition to the ROI calculator that we provided in Chapter 3, organizations must track a variety of metrics that quantify its influence. As you increase the eminence of your thought leadership program, your organization's leaders will want to know who is consuming your content, how it's impacting their decisions, and, perhaps most importantly, whether it has piqued their interest in the products and services your parent organization provides.

To satisfy these requests, your team will need to define and establish KPIs that, when taken together, tell a story about how your content is being consumed and what actions it has inspired. Clear, quantifiable measurements reported on a regular cadence will help demonstrate the value of thought leadership as a key part of your organization's go-to-market strategy.

The ROI of thought leadership should be used front and center in any performance report for your organization, as this figure will showcase why thought leadership should be the foundation for other, less lucrative, promotion activities. However, tracking and sharing a wider set

Table 11.1 Measures of thought leadership quality.

Metric	Internal (organization), external (market), or both	Description
Time on page	Both	This tells you how long people spend, on average, consuming your content by staying on your website – and how much time they're willing to invest to hear what you have to say.
Downloads	Both	Most thought leadership can be downloaded from a digital platform. How many times a piece of content is downloaded can tell you whether people find it valuable enough to share it with others, reference it in their own work, or investigate it more fully later.
Social media likes	External	A social media "like" is just one step beyond lurking, but this metric helps you gauge overall interest in your content on social platforms. The more targeted your follower audience, the more valuable this metric will be.
Social media shares	External	When people share your content with others in their social media networks, it tells you they liked it so much that they want others to experience it for themselves. This is a step up from simply liking your posts and demonstrates that your audience believes that your thought leadership can help them build their personal eminence.

of metrics can highlight the broad scope of business benefits this valuable investment delivers.

Quality Metrics

How is your audience engaging with your content? How long do they spend consuming it? Are they sharing it with colleagues, their professional networks, or their teams? Is the media reporting on the data and insights you've published?

Although there are numerous ways to measure thought leadership quality, which is largely subjective, we've identified four key performance indicators (KPIs) that can help you gauge the caliber of your content.

Uniqueness Metrics

Is your content transactional or have you built relationships with your audience that keep them coming back for more? Does your audience find the content engaging, unique, and valuable? Does it influence their purchasing or spending decisions? Are other parts of your organization using the thought leadership to build or deepen relationships with their customers?

Uniqueness measures tell you whether you have a differentiated message – and how well it is aligned to business goals. Here are five specific KPIs you can use to gauge how strongly your content resonates with your target audience.

Reach Metrics

Is your thought leadership credible, authoritative, and in-demand? Is it seen as independent by those in your

Table 11.2 Measures of thought leadership uniqueness.

Metric	Internal (organization), external (market), or both	Description
Subscriptions	Both	Because subscribers self-select, this metric helps you gauge the size of your most-loyal user base, whether clients and prospects or co-workers on account and sales teams. When this number grows, it could be a sign that your content is hitting the right mark.
Net Promoter Score (NPS)	Mostly external, but could be used internally as well.	NPS is a very simple one-question survey, answered on a 10-point scale, that measures a user's likelihood to recommend a product or service. It is widely used to measure loyalty and satisfaction and can give you a good sense of whether your audience, either clients and prospects, or co-workers on account and sales teams, feels your content is relevant and valuable.

Instances of thought leadership use by account teams	Internal	Account leaders are typically busy people, so if they use your content to spark client conversations, they must find it compelling. Tracking the number of times your thought leadership is used by account teams can gauge its uniqueness and serve as a proxy for how frequently clients are exposed to your content.
Deals or requests for proposal (RFPs) explicitly referencing thought leadership	Internal	How frequently account teams use thought leadership in client pitches can also help you gauge the relevance and alignment of your content. These references directly connect thought leadership to business conversations. You can gather this information by surveying client-facing colleagues.
Thought leadership rankings	External	Source Global Research[1] regularly ranks thought leadership–producing organizations. It evaluates programs based on several criteria, including depth of analysis, originality, relevance, and usability. Earning a top spot in these independent rankings signals that your organization is creating unique, differentiated thought leadership content.

(Continued)

181

Table 11.2 (Continued)

Metric	Internal (organization), external (market), or both	Description
Thought leadership awards	External	The value of winning awards can be debated, but if nothing else, it is a point of pride and rewards the teams producing the content. There are many thought leadership recognition programs, including The Stevie Awards (https://stevieawards.com), which introduced its thought leadership category for the first time in 2022; and MomentumITSMA (https://momentumitsma.com/marketing-excellence-awards), which also has a specific thought leadership category.
Invitations to present at conferences and events	External	Tracking the number of times your team is invited to speak at in-person or virtual events tells you how relevant organizers think you are to their audiences. They won't invite you unless they think your organization's brand or the title of your content will help attract attendees. Collect this information by sending a simple survey to thought leadership colleagues – and remind them to include the invitations they've declined as well as those they've accepted.

Table 11.3 Measures of thought leadership reach.

Metric	Internal (organization), external (market), or both	Description
Views	Both	This metric tells you how many times a piece of content has been viewed on digital channels. Most analytics tools will let you measure total views and unique views – the number of net-new individuals who viewed the content within a given time frame.
Media mentions	External	When press articles feature data or insights from your thought leadership, it introduces your content to new and broader audiences. Smaller organizations can estimate this metric by searching for your organization's name or recent study titles using Google's "news" filter. Larger organizations might contract with a formal reporting service that collects and summarizes media mentions.
Incoming media inquiries	External	Authoritative thought leadership can provide reporters easy access to data, direct quotes, and business insight that can make their jobs easier. Whether a result of a media pitch or organic visibility, measuring incoming media inquiries can gauge the newsworthiness of your content – and the credibility of your brand in the business community.

target audience? Are you capturing and keeping the attention of existing and prospective clients and customers?

Reach metrics tell you whether your thought leadership is asking the right questions – and if your findings are relevant to the market. Explore three KPIs that can help you determine whether your thought leadership is building buzz for your brand.

As with other business initiatives, the best way to sustain support for thought leadership is to clearly demonstrate the value it creates. But that hasn't always been easy. For some organizations, investing in thought leadership has been a leap of faith – or a response to FOMO (fear of missing out). That is changing. With the ROI methodology and supplementary KPIs contained in this book, thought leadership–producing organizations can prove once and for all that thought leadership does generate value – and accurately measure their slice of the thought leadership pie: $100 billion in the United States and $265 billion globally.

Chapter 12

The Thought Leadership Multiplier Effect

Thought leadership delivers value by building relationships with clients, business partners, the media, and the public. For these relationships to generate the greatest ROI, they must be anchored on trust – and your organization's reputation for developing robust, rigorous, and relevant content.

That means each piece of thought leadership you produce should strengthen this reputation, tapping into the research, analysis, and business insights that make your organization's point of view unique. What's more, your content should connect. Rather than existing as individual stars in the sky, each thought leadership report should form constellations that bring your organization's point of view to life.

What does that look like? It starts with taking a portfolio approach to thought leadership – looking at publication calendar from 30,000 feet. This streamlines the daily work of content creation, as it's much easier to craft multiple pieces from a single study than conduct original research for every piece you produce. But that's just the beginning.

By weaving a tapestry of content that ranges from snackable to scrupulous, you can draw more people in, hold their attention longer, and inspire them to come back more frequently. While content can be sliced and diced in any number of ways, a hub-and-spoke thought leadership strategy can create a multiplier effect.

This approach starts with a big idea – the inspiration at the center of your content strategy. Your big idea will inform your research hypothesis and provide a focal point for your analysis and core narrative. Extender content creates stickiness and boosts engagement by showcasing your findings in different lights. Defender content protects your turf by going deeper into the details. By preparing your thought leadership for different content formats, distribution channels, and audience segments, you can start to see much bigger returns from your thought leadership investment. Let's explore each of these content types in more detail.

Big Ideas

Putting thought leadership's big ideas at the top of the brand funnel can create a virtuous environment that increases value exponentially. It lets content cascade from the top to inform campaign initiatives across the enterprise.

Focusing your content strategy on big ideas that you can franchise – meaning they will inspire a broad set of extender and defender assets – can generate and maintain powerful multiplier effects. While a thought leadership report might be generally relevant in its original form, it can become uniquely captivating when coupled with extender and defender assets. Highlighting data and insights targeted directly to specific industries, regions, or roles can dramatically increase your content's relatability and relevance.

Using one major thought leadership investment to inspire scores of derivative pieces can be an especially useful for smaller thought leadership organizations that don't have the resources or budgets to conduct more frequent original research. For example, the Project Management Institute conducts major research studies on the value that the formal practice of project management delivers to organizations (see The Pulse of the Profession®).[1] The original report in this franchise, concepted by one of this book's authors in 2012, was titled *The High Cost of Low Performance*. This original piece was arresting enough to generate ongoing attention across several extender pieces, such as geographic and industry-specific reports. And more than a decade later, the franchise still serves as the foundation of the organization's thought leadership program.

Like other *big idea* assets, a content franchise can generate brand and market impact in the form of a lengthy coverage period with a substantial number of media hits – along with increased requests for interviews – in targeted outlets. It generates customer returns in the form of new conversations with senior decision makers and follow-on meetings with their delegates. And it keeps internal account teams happy because they know they can expect regular updates within this franchise to share with their clients and prospects.

There are six main reasons why a thought leadership program centered on big ideas works effectively:

1. It creates clear parameters that help your organization create content that is strategically aligned and customer oriented.

2. It coalesces attention and resources around market-shaping ideas that can deliver tangible value to key audiences.

3. It offers opportunities to extend thought leadership investments across the organization and down through the marketing funnel.

4. It increases business and customer value with each extension, giving audiences an increasingly well-rounded understanding of the issue at hand.

5. It lets your organization demonstrate continued mastery of a given subject from more vantage points.

6. It leverages efficiencies of knowledge, reach, and scale.

If your research is not structured to allow for the creation of extender and defender content, you should reconsider how you are conducting your surveys. The first step is to ensure you are collecting enough responses from a wide variety of individuals that are representative of your most important clients or customers. That way, you can extend the life and value of your research investment – and tap the content channels and formats that are most likely to engage different target audiences.

Extender Content

Within the context of a successful big idea franchise, extender assets are derivative content pieces that make the anchor asset more relevant to specific sub-markets or communities.

Extender content can increase the impact of your thought leadership by earning placements in relevant trade and market media outlets and spurring speaking opportunities at industry or community-specific events. For example, Deloitte's *Navigating the new digital divide,*[2] which focuses on the impact of digital technologies in the retail market, is a global point of view summarizing data from nine specific countries. Deloitte also published individual reports for each country, and lists these extender pieces on its website.

Examples of extender content include:

- Industry- or region-specific versions of the original report or research findings.
- Content that highlights relevant findings for clearly defined sub-audiences, such as particular job roles or functions or businesses of different sizes.
- A series of "by the numbers" charts or graphs.
- Marketing case studies that feature your organization's products and client testimonials.
- "Voice of the client" interviews or Q&As.
- Implementation models or tools.
- Byline media articles or an authored column on owned social channels, such as in Medium or LinkedIn.

The variety of extender content types is limited only by your team's time, imagination, and budget, as long as your data sample is large enough to be cut in several different ways. And in the age of generative AI, a few well-written prompts can turn your original data into clever derivative content in a matter of minutes. Remember to share your data carefully, however, understanding that generative AI tools may capture the information you share and use it in the outputs it creates for others.

Defender Content

Defender content takes a different tack. Instead of going wider, it takes your content deeper. To guard against competitors gaining authority on a specific topic, this content gets granular, leaving no stone unturned. Continuing the story that started with your big idea makes it harder for competitors to jump into the conversation and present themselves as experts. Defender content reminds your audience that you were the first to conduct this research – and that your analysis remains the best.

Examples of defender content include:

- Deep dive studies that leverage additional survey data to reveal more detailed and specific insights.

- Opinion or point-of-view pieces on related topics that incorporate data and insights from your original big idea study. These pieces are often published as blog posts, *Medium* articles, or LinkedIn posts.

- Supplementary content that includes new information obtained through client interviews, additional pulse surveys that assess potential market shifts of any changes in perception, or any new thinking that has emerged in the field since the original piece was published.

- Data visualizations that highlight the depth of your findings, perhaps showing how perspectives or behaviors have changed over the lifetime of your big idea franchise.

Defender assets can generate interest and loyalty by demonstrating relevance while denying others exclusivity. New outputs can amplify your "drumbeat" – or ongoing publication strategy. The IBM Institute for Business Value took this approach with *The CEO's Guide to Generative AI*. The anchor "big idea" study explored the state of the market[3] while the defender pieces dived deeply into multiple business areas[4] being impacted by generative AI, incorporating new research that informed function-specific insights.

Chapter 13

The Value of Thought Leadership, Quantified. Finally.

This book has built a clear business case for thought leadership – but knowing how to deliver value is only half the battle. Building a successful thought leadership–producing organization takes time, attention, expertise, innovation, investment, and continued support from executive sponsors.

Yet, when it's successful, thought leadership can yield dramatic benefits that are well worth the effort. We have demonstrated that conservatively, thought leadership is a $100 billion opportunity – and even small organizations can capture a sizable share.

Emerging technologies, in particular generative AI, are making content creation faster and easier than ever. But how organizations tap this technology will likely differentiate thought leaders from thought followers in the future. When used properly, it could accelerate speed to insight, helping organizations beat the competition to market. On the other hand, if it's used by the untrained, inexperienced, or uninvested, generative AI could devolve thought leadership into drivel.

To get the greatest possible returns on thought leadership, your organization must embrace it as a strategic capability – and position it as the 8th P of marketing: the platform that supports all other enterprise promotions and outreach programs. We've outlined all the ingredients you need in the mix, from strategy and alignment to operating model and measurement. All that's left is the baking. Rally your talent and resources, skills, and creativity today – and start telling the stories only your organization can tell.

Notes

Introduction

1 Hall, John, "Is Thought Leadership Everything It's Cracked Up to Be?," *Forbes*, November 3, 2019, https://www.forbes.com/sites/johnhall/ 2019/11/03/is-thought-leadership-everything-its-cracked-up-to-be/?sh=53560ade9341. Accessed 3 July 2024.

2 Park, Chang, "Maximize the Return on Your Advertising Spend," *Nielsen*, December 2009, https://www.nielsen.com/insights/2009/ maximize-the-return-on-your-advertising-spend/. Accessed 3 July 2024.

3 "Marketing Mix," *Wikipedia*, https://en.wikipedia.org/wiki/Marketing_ mix. Accessed 2 July 2024.

Chapter 2

1 ChatGPT Prompt: *Why can't generative AI create thought leadership?* Answer: *Generative AI can produce text that appears to be thought leadership, but it lacks the ability to truly understand the concepts it is writing about. Thought leadership requires a deep understanding of a field, the ability to synthesize information from multiple sources, and the capacity to generate new and valuable insights. While generative AI is excellent at processing large amounts of data and identifying patterns, it lacks the creativity and intuition that humans possess. It is limited by the data it has been trained on and cannot generate truly original ideas or insights. Furthermore, thought leadership is not just about the output of ideas or insights, but also about the process of developing those ideas. It involves*

critical thinking, collaboration, and debate, which are all human activities that cannot be replicated by AI. In short, while generative AI can produce text that appears to be thought leadership, it lacks the true understanding and creativity required to generate genuine thought leadership. Accessed 14 October 2023, https://chatgpt. com/c/35598391-84cd-44f0-9094-3ac9c2d13365.

2 Park. "Return on Advertising Spend."

3 Rex Briggs and Greg Stuart, *What Sticks: Why Most Advertising Fails and How to Guarantee Yours Succeeds* (Kaplan Business 2006).

4 Park. "Return on Advertising Spend."

Chapter 4

1 Dammann, Luc. "Demand for content shows no sign of slowing." *Adobe blog.* March 21, 2023. https://blog.adobe.com/en/publish/ 2023/03/21/adobe-research-demand-for-content-shows-no-sign-of-slowing. Accessed 3 July 2024.

2 ChatGPT, accessed 14 October 2023.

3 McGann, James G., "2020 Global Go To Think Tank Index Report," *University of Pennsylvania Scholarly Commons.* According to the University of Pennsylvania, there are 11,175 think tanks globally – ranging from foreign policy to environment to technology. If we assume each publishes one TL paper every month, it would equate to 11,175 × 12 or about ~135,000 pieces of thought leadership every year. https://www.bruegel.org/sites/default/files/wp-content/uploads/ 2021/03/2020-Global-Go-To-Think-Tank-Index-Report-Bruegel.pdf.

4 Emily Field, Alexis Krivkovich, Sandra Kügele, Nicole Robinson, and Lareina Yee, "Women in the Workplace 2023," *McKinsey & Company,* 5 October 2023 https://www.mckinsey.com/featured-insights/diversity-and-inclusion/women-in-the-workplace. Accessed 3 July 2024.

5 Global Thought Leadership Institute at APQC, https://www.apqc. org/GTLI.

6 Based on "Quality Ratings of Thought Leadership for 2024," White Space rankings of thought leadership quality by Source Global, full report available to White Space subscribers. https://www.sourceglobalresearch.com/reports/9498-quality-ratings-of-thought-leadership-for-2024. Accessed 3 July 2024.

7 Muqsit Ashraf, Rachel Barton, Olivier Schunck, and Bill Theofilou, "Strategy at the pace of technology," *Accenture*, https://www.accenture.com/us-en/insights/strategy/strategy-pace-technology. Accessed 3 July 2024.

8 Axel Schmidt, Johannes Trenka, Dr. Maximilian Holtgrave, and Tobias Büchsenschütz, "Electric vehicles on the rise: Why new-car sales and aftersales are set for a radical transformation – and what automakers and dealers can do now, *Accenture*, https://www.accenture.com/content/dam/accenture/final/a-com-migration/r3-3/pdf/pdf-179/accenture-electric-vehicles-on-the-rise.pdf. Accessed 3 July 2024.

9 Salima Lin, Kelly Chambliss, Kitty Chaney Reed, Carolyn Childers, Lindsay Kaplan, Nickle LaMoreaux, Lula Mohanty, Paul Papas, Carla Grant-Pickens, Joanne Wright, Carolyn Heller Baird, and Cindy Anderson, "Women in Leadership: Why Perception Outpaces the Pipeline and What to Do About It," *IBM Institute for Business Value*, 8 March 2023, https://www.ibm.com/thought-leadership/institute-business-value/en-us/report/women-leadership-2023. Accessed 3 July 2024.

10 Salima Lin, Joanne Wright, Yvonne Li, and Debra D'Agostino, "Forging the Future of AI: Women Can Take the Lead," *IBM Institute for Business Value*, 6 March 2024, https://www.ibm.com/thought-leadership/institute-business-value/en-us/report/women-leadership-ai. Accessed 3 July 2024.

11 John Granger, Jesus Mantas, and Salima Lin, "Seven Bets: It's Time to Bet on the Future," *IBM Institute for Business Value*, 8 May 2023, https://www.ibm.com/thought-leadership/institute-business-value/en-us/report/seven-bets. Accessed 3 July 2024.

12 Chris McCurdy, Shlomi Kramer, Gerald Parham, and Jacob Dencik, Ph.D, "Prosper in the Cyber Economy," *IBM Institute for Business Value*, 14 November 2022, https://www.ibm.com/thought-leadership/institute-business-value/en-us/report/security-cyber-economy. Accessed 3 July 2024.

13 "Global Climate Risk Barometer: When Will Climate Disclosures Start to Impact Decarbonization?" *EY*, September 2022, https://assets.ey.com/content/dam/ey-sites/ey-com/en_gl/topics/climate-change/ey-global-climate-risk-barometer-report-v2.pdf. Accessed 3 July 2024.

14 Eric Melloul, Ben Black, Jean-Charles van den Branden, and Magali Deryckere, "Purpose-led Brands Can Reshape the Consumer Goods Industry if they can Scale," *Bain & Co*, 29 October 2022, https://www.bain.com/insights/purpose-led-brands-can-reshape-the-consumer-goods-industry-if-they-can-scale/. Accessed 3 July 2024.

15 Jan Mischke, Chris Bradley, Marc Canal, Olivia White, Sven Smit, and Denitsa Georgieva, "Investing in Productivity Growth," *McKinsey & Company*, 27 March 2024, https://www.mckinsey.com/mgi/our-research/investing-in-productivity-growth. Accessed 3 July 2024.

16 "Global Threat Assessment 2023, *WeProtect Global Alliance and PA Consulting*, https://www.weprotect.org/global-threat-assessment-23. Accessed 3 July 2024.

Chapter 7

1 Bernd Heid, Martin Linder, and Mark Patel, "Delivering the Climate Technologies Needed for Net Zero," *McKinsey & Company*, 18 April 2022. https://www.mckinsey.com/capabilities/sustainability/our-insights/delivering-the-climate-technologies-needed-for-net-zero. Accessed 3 July 2024.

2 *Source Global*, "Quality Ratings."

3 "2024 Edelman Trust Barometer: Innovation in Peril," *Edelman*, https://www.edelman.com/trust/trust-barometer. Accessed 3 July 2024.

4 "People Manifesto," *Brightline Initiative*, https://www.brightline. org/people-manifesto/. Accessed 3 July 2024.

5 "UAE Future 2030–2117," *The United Arab Emirates Government Portal*, Updated 4 January 2024, https://u.ae/en/more/uae-future/ 2030-2117. Accessed 3 July 2024.

Chapter 8

1 Annie Murphy Paul, "Your Brain on Fiction," *New York Times*, 18 March 2012. https://www.nytimes.com/2012/03/18/opinion/ sunday/the-neuroscience-of-your-brain-on-fiction.html? pagewanted=all. Accessed 3 July 2024.

2 Paul, "Brain on Fiction."

3 Paul Zak, "How Stories Change the Brain," *Greater Good Magazine*, The University of California, Berkeley, 17 December 2013, https:// greatergood.berkeley.edu/article/item/how_stories_change_brain. Accessed 3 July 2024.

4 Lin, et al., "Women in Leadership."

5 Caroline Baum, "Interview: Elizabeth Strout," *The Sydney Morning Herald*, 29 June 2013, www.smh.com.au/entertainment/books/ interview-elizabeth-strout-20130627-2oy6t.html. Accessed 3 July 2024.

6 "The First Draft of Anything Is Shit," *Quote Investigator*, 20 September 2015, https://quoteinvestigator.com/2015/09/20/draft. Accessed 3 July 2024.

7 Anne Trafton, "In the blink of an eye," *MIT News Office*, March 2014. https://news.mit.edu/2014/in-the-blink-of-an-eye-0116#:~: text=However%2C%20a%20team%20of%20neuroscientists, milliseconds%20suggested%20by%20previous%20studies. Accessed 3 July 2024.

8 *Visual Capitalist*, Creator Program, https://www.visualcapitalist. com/creator-hub. Accessed 3 July 2024.

Chapter 9

1 Krystal Hu, "ChatGPT sets record for fastest-growing user base – analyst note," *Reuters*, 2 February 2023, https://www.reuters.com/technology/chatgpt-sets-record-fastest-growing-user-base-analyst-note-2023-02-01. Accessed 4 July 2024.

2 "Enterprise Generative AI: State of the Market," *IBM Institute for Business Value*, 12 July 2023, https://www.ibm.com/thought-leadership/institute-business-value/en-us/report/enterprise-generative-ai. Accessed 4 July 2024.

3 Justin Ablett, Carolyn Heller Baird, Jay Trestain, Tammy Pienknagura, Chris Blandy, and Rachael Barnett, "The revolutionary content supply chain: How generative AI supercharges creativity and productivity," *IBM Institute for Business Value*, March 2024, https://www.ibm.com/thought-leadership/institute-business-value/en-us/report/content-supply-chain. Accessed 4 July 2024.

4 David Dodd, "Why Generative AI Can't Create Real Thought Leadership Content … At Least Not Yet," *Customer Think*, 24 May 2023, https://customerthink.com/why-generative-ai-cant-create-real-thought-leadership-content-at-least-not-yet. Accessed 4 July 2024.

5 Chloe Veltman, "Thousands of Authors urge AI companies to stop using work without permission," *NPR, Morning Edition*, 17 July 2023, https://www.npr.org/2023/07/17/1187523435/thousands-of-authors-urge-ai-companies-to-stop-using-work-without-permission. Accessed 4 July 2024.

6 Mike Hayes, Amy Matsuo, Arun Ghosh, Katherine Blue, Tegan Keele, Pravin Chandran, and Alistair Hall, "The Decarbonization Journey: Five Pillars to Achieving Net Zero," *KPMG*, June 2021, https://assets.kpmg.com/content/dam/kpmg/dp/pdf/2021/june/decarbonization-journey.pdf. Accessed 4 July 2024.

7 Ablett, et al., "Content Supply Chain."

8 Source Global, "Quality Ratings."

9 "2024 Edelman Trust Barometer."

10 Ben Sisario, "Jann Wenner's Rock Hall Reign Lasted Years. It Ended in 20 Minutes." *New York Times*, 19 September 2023, https://www.nytimes.com/2023/09/19/arts/music/jann-wenner-rock-and-roll-hall-of-fame.html. Accessed 4 July 2024.

Chapter 10

1 A 2006 study published in HBR found that CEOs spend 21% of their time directly engaging with direct reports – and they work on average, 9.7 hours per day. This means that in a typical five-day week, CEOs work on average 48.5 hours. Of which, engagement with direct reports comprises 10.2 hours weekly. Another recent HBR article estimates that a typical CEO has 10 individuals reporting to them directly, which implies that a typical CEO spends approximately 1 hour per week engaging with each direct report. See: https://hbr.org/2018/07/how-ceos-manage-time and https://hbr.org/2012/04/how-many-direct-reports. Accessed 20 September 2023.

2 https://www.businessmole.com/13-of-the-best-press-release-distribution-services-2019 and https://www.thesmbguide.com/free-press-release-distribution-services. Accessed 20 September 2023.

3 Katie Sehl and Karolina Mikolajczyk, "Engagement Rate Calculator + Tips for 2024," *Hootsuite*, 20 March 2024 https://blog.hootsuite.com/calculate-engagement-rate/#:~:text=Most%20social%20media%20marketing%20experts,well%20your%20accounts%20are%20doing. Accessed 4 July 2024.

4 "Ultimate Email Marketing Benchmarks for 2022: By Industry and Day," *Campaign Monitor*, https://www.campaignmonitor.com/resources/guides/email-marketing-benchmarks. Accessed 4 July 2024.

5 "Email Marketing Benchmarks and Metrics Businesses Should Track," *Intuit Mail Chimp*, https://mailchimp.com/resources/email-marketing-benchmarks. Accessed 4 July 2024.

6 Koba Molenaar, "23 Podcast Statistics You Should Know in 2023," *Influencer Marketing Hub*, 19 July 2023, https://influencermarket inghub.com/podcast-statistics. Accessed 4 July 2024.

7 BCG "Imagine This" podcast: https://link.chtbl.com/imagine-this-Wallenstein-CEO?sid=ceo-articlesum-ep5. Accessed 24 July 2024.

8 Rohit Shewale, "Webinar Statistics in 2024 (Attendance Rate & More)," *Demand Sage*, https://www.demandsage.com/webinar-statistics Accessed 20 September 2023.

9 Shewale, "Webinar Statistics." Accessed 4 July 2024.

10 "The Ultimate Webinar Benchmarks and Best Practices Report for 2022," *Deck7*, 19 August 2022, https://deck7.com/blog/the-ultimate-webinar-benchmarks-and-best-practices-report-for-2022#:~:text=According%20to%20ON24%2C%20if%20the,has%20a%20better%20attendance%20rate. Accessed 24 July 2024.

11 Paper and Packaging Board, "The Revenge of Print," *LinkedIn*, https://www.linkedin.com/pulse/revenge-print-paper-and-packaging-board-linee/?trackingId=qPoT%2BNZf926%2FMKEyK8Je VA%3D%3D. Accessed 4 July 2024.

12 The Brightline Initiative, *Project Management Institute*, https://www.brightline.org/resources/books. Accessed 4 July 2024.

13 Anthony Marshall, Cindy Anderson, Christian Bieck, and Carolyn Heller Baird, "The CEO's Guide to Generative AI – Marketing," *IBM Institute for Business Value*, 5 December 2023, https://www.ibm.com/thought-leadership/institute-business-value/en-us/report/ceo-generative-ai/ceo-ai-marketing. Accessed 24 July 2024.

Chapter 11

1 "Quality Ratings." *Source Global*.

Chapter 12

1 "Pulse of the Profession, "Project Management Institute, https://www.pmi.org/learning/thought-leadership/pulse. Accessed 24 July 2024.

2 Navigating the new digital divide: Global edition, *Deloitte*, https://www2.deloitte.com/tr/en/pages/consumer-business/articles/gx-global-digital-divide-retail.html. Accessed 24 July 2024.

3 "The CEO's Guide to Generative AI," *IBM Institute for Business Value*, https://www.ibm.com/thought-leadership/institute-business-value/en-us/report/ceo-generative-ai. Accessed 24 July 2024.

4 "The CEO's Guide." *IBM Institute for Business Value.*

Survey Methodology

Total number of C-suite executives surveyed globally that informed the analysis contained in this book comprised 4,016.

First, in collaboration with Oxford Economics, we conducted a series of three surveys of thought leadership consumers, totaling 3,716 executives, from May 2021 through February 2022.

Demographic breakdown:

6 C-suite roles
Chief Executive Officer (CEO) – 50%
Chief Information Officer (CIO) – 15%
Chief Technology Officer (CTOs) – 15%
Chief Financial Officer (CFO) – 10%
Chief Supply Chain Officer (CSCO) – 5%
Chief Operations Officer (COO) – 5%

16 countries
Australia – 4%
Brazil – 4%
Canada – 4%
China – 7%
France – 4%
Germany – 7%
India – 7%
Italy – 4%

Japan – 7%
Mexico – 4%
Singapore – 4%
South Africa – 4%
South Korea – 4%
Switzerland – 4%
United Kingdom – 7%
United States – 25%

20 industries

Agriculture – 3%
Automotive (Original Equipment Manufacturers [OEMs] and Suppliers) – 6%
Banking – 10%
Chemicals – 3%
Consumer Products – 6%
Education – 4%
Electronics – 5%
Federal (or National) and State Government – 9%
Financial Markets – 4%
Healthcare (providers and payers) – 4%
Information Technology (IT) – 5%
Insurance – 4%
Life Sciences and Pharmaceuticals – 3%
Manufacturing – 8%
Media and Entertainment – 4%
Petroleum – 2%
Retail – 6%
Telecommunications – 5%
Travel and Transportation – 5%
Energy and Utilities – 4%

Organization size

Average annual revenue was $14 billion across all 3,382 non-government organizations globally. In the United States specifically, average annual organization revenue came to $29 billion.

Data collection methods

Data was gathered through one-on-one phone or online interviews with respondents, based on a detailed questionnaire developed by the authors. Interviews were double-blind, which means that interviewees weren't told who initiated the research and we are unable to trace who specifically was interviewed from what organization.

Demographic data on both the interviewee and their organization was reported anonymously, which enables detailed, comprehensive, and unbiased analysis. For multiple choice response questions, answer options were randomized. In addition to the surveys of thought leadership users, the authors conducted one-on-one interviews with more than a dozen leading thought leadership producers on topics ranging from their objectives and strategies to how they operationalize thought leadership and the metrics they use to measure success.

Second, in May and June 2023, we surveyed an additional 300 US-based C-suite leaders to better understand how generative AI is impacting their perception toward and consumption of thought leadership. One hundred fifty of the executives surveyed were CEOs, with the other 150 distributed equally between CIOs/CTOs, CMOs, and CFOs. Respondents were located in the United States and represented 19 industries. Average organization size of those surveyed was $18 billion in annual revenue.

Acknowledgments

We would like to thank a few people who supported this journey, including Salima Lin, Peter Korsten, Jacob Dencik, Steve Ballou, Raj Teer, Tegan Jones, Kristin Biron, and Marie Glenn. We also deeply appreciate the support of our families: Cary and Chay Anderson, Shirley Petersen, and Tawatchai Promrat.

About the Authors

Cindy Anderson is the Chief Marketing Officer/Global Lead for Engagement & Eminence at the IBM Institute for Business Value (IBV). She has co-authored research reports, published numerous articles, and delivered presentations on thought leadership, diversity, strategy implementation, project management, and technology to global audiences. She oversees a team of 30 editors, designers, and social media/email marketers. She is a founding board member of the Global Thought Leadership Institute at APQC, a new association that advances the practice of thought leadership. More detail is available on LinkedIn at: https://www .linkedin.com/in/clwanderson480.

Anthony Marshall is Senior Research Director of thought leadership at the IBM Institute for Business Value (IBV), leading the top-rated thought leadership and analysis program. He oversees a global team of 60 technology and industry experts, statisticians, economists, and analysts. Anthony conducts original thought leadership and has authored dozens of refereed articles and studies on topics including generative AI, innovation, digital and business transformation and ecosystems, open collaboration, and skills. He speaks at numerous conferences and events each year. He is a founding board member of the Global Thought Leadership Institute at APQC, a new association that advances the practice of thought leadership. More detail is available on LinkedIn at: https://www.linkedin.com/in/anthonyejmarshall.

Index

215